The Kingdom of Heaven

The Kingdom of Heaven

A Devotional Commentary on the Discourses of Jesus in Matthew

Edward B. Allen

Melbourne

The Kingdom of Heaven: A Devotional Commentary on the Discourses of Jesus in Matthew
by Edward B. Allen
Copyright © 2019 by Edward B. Allen
All rights reserved worldwide.
Reprinted with revisions, 2020, 2021, 2026.

Published by Edward B. Allen
Melbourne, Florida
Email: edward.allen1949@gmail.com

ISBN: 978-1-7320708-5-1 (paperback)
978-1-7320708-6-8 (ebook *.epub)
978-1-7320708-7-5 (Kindle ebook *.mobi)

Cover design by Ken Raney (http://kenraney.com).

To Angie

Contents

Contents

Contents

Preface

The Kingdom of Heaven is a popular topic among Christian preachers and theologians. Some emphasize the return of Jesus to Planet Earth when his reign will be established over all. Others emphasize service to mankind today as the way to express Kingdom values. Some cults have tried to establish the Kingdom on earth by their own efforts. What did Jesus say about the Kingdom of Heaven?

This book emphasizes personal applications for daily life from Jesus' direct teaching about the Kingdom of Heaven. If I will understand and do what Jesus said about the Kingdom of Heaven, then I will benefit in this life and in eternity. Instead of analyzing theology, this book consists of passage-by-passage devotional comments on the five discourses of Jesus in Matthew's gospel. Other Scriptures are discussed where relevant. The illustrations are based on the recollections of actual people and events by friends, family, or myself unless otherwise indicated.

You may also want to read traditional commentaries which address other concerns, such as textual variants of manuscripts, translation issues, cultural context, and alternative interpretations. Even though this is not an academic book, I have benefited greatly from Christian scholars. Some word translations, cultural notes, and interpretations come from a commentary by D. A. Carson,[1] who is an evangelical Bible scholar. I hope you will read his commentary for yourself. Unfortunately, it is not practical to cite all the pastors and books from whom I have gleaned over the years.

The Christian Standard Bible (CSB) is quoted as the primary translation. It is a modern translation based on the latest evangelical Bible scholarship. There are some quotes from other translations as well. Clarifications of quotations are in [brackets]. Scripture references consist of book, chapter, verses, and version (if relevant), for example, "John 3:16 (KJV)" for the King James Version of the Bible. When Matthew is referenced, the book is omitted, for example, "5:3 (CSB)."

Epigraphs at the beginning of each chapter are quotations from *The Cost of Discipleship* by Dietrich Bonhoeffer.[2] A word or phrase referred to as a word is

---

[1] D. A. Carson, "Matthew," *The Expositor's Bible Commentary: Matthew, Mark, Luke*, Vol. 8, (Grand Rapids, Michigan: Zondervan, 1990).

[2] Dietrich Bonhoeffer, *The Cost of Discipleship* (revised ed.), translated by R. H. Fuller (New York: Macmillan, 1963). First edition in German, *Nachfolge*, 1937.

in *italics*. Male pronouns are sometimes used to indicate a person of either gender. Transliterated Hebrew and Greek words are also in *italics*, mostly in notes. Hebrew and Greek definitions are from Strong's *Exhaustive Concordance of the Bible*. Strong's reference numbers for Hebrew and Greek words are used rather than full citations, for example, "(*Strong's* No. 2346)." Addresses of Web sites are followed by dates when they were valid, for example, "(Current March 1, 2019)." All Scripture references and section titles are indexed.

I thank Helen Badger and Ron Chambers for their helpful comments. I am also thankful for the steadfast support of my wife, Angie.

E.B.A.

1

The Kingdom of Heaven

In Jesus Christ his followers have witnessed the kingdom of God breaking in on earth.

Dietrich Bonhoeffer[1]

The Kingdom of Heaven was not just an academic topic for the disciples. They did not conduct conferences about God's reign. They saw Jesus defeat disease, demons, and death. The Kingdom had come to earth.

My life was going on from day to day, but God surprised me when the Kingdom of Heaven invaded my life and the lives of those around me. A life was transformed by the gospel. A compulsive behavior pattern went away after a demon was cast out.

Hansel was an alcoholic.[2] His life was in ruins, but he responded to the gospel, committed his life to Jesus, and was instantly delivered from his addiction. God restored his life.

In the middle of a conversation, Angie's associate pastor suddenly cast a demon out of her.[3] She felt it go. Afterwards, she noticed that she no longer reacted compulsively to repetitive noises.

When Jesus was on earth, he healed the sick, cast out demons, and raised the dead. His disciples saw what he did. Jesus spoke of the Kingdom of Heaven many times. One of his disciples, named Matthew, wrote down what Jesus said about the Kingdom. This book is a devotional study of five extensive passages in the Gospel of Matthew where Jesus explained the Kingdom of Heaven. The goal is to understand the Kingdom and to apply his teaching to modern life.

---

[1]Bonhoeffer, p. 184.

[2]Edward B. Allen, *Love, Sex, Money, and Power: A Devotional Commentary* (Melbourne, Florida: Edward B. Allen, 2017), p. 109.

[3]Edward B. Allen, *Love, Sex, Money, and Power*, p. 110.

The Kingdom

A *kingdom* is defined as a domain ruled by a king. For example, my backyard is surrounded by a fence. It is my domain. It is my job to tend it. The neighbor's shrubs are trying to come through the fence, and the weeds sure grow fast. I need to manage this corner of God's creation better.

Modern nations are kingdoms, even though they may not call their leaders *kings*. Too often corruption, selfishness, dishonesty, and incompetence of leaders make a mess of things. The Kingdom of Heaven must be a better place.

Is the Kingdom of Heaven like a human kingdom? Can I see it? When I read the news, I'm often outraged at the evils taking place in this world. It sure would be nice if I could move somewhere that's run righteously. Can I move to the Kingdom of Heaven?

> Being asked by the Pharisees when the kingdom of God would come, [Jesus] answered them, "The kingdom of God is not coming with something observable; no one will say, 'See here!' or 'There!' For you see, the kingdom of God is in your midst."
>
> Luke 17:20–21 (CSB)

The Jews of Jesus' time were looking for a human king who would free them from Rome. Jesus told them the Kingdom of Heaven is not that kind of kingdom. It is inside of people. During his trial, Pilate asked Jesus if he was King of the Jews. Jesus told Pilate the Kingdom is not of this world.[4] Pilate was surprised, but soon realized the Kingdom of Heaven has a spiritual dimension.

Who is the king? What will his reign be like?

> For a child will be born for us,
> a son will be given to us,
> and the government will be on his shoulders.
> He will be named
> Wonderful Counselor, Mighty God,
> Eternal Father, Prince of Peace.
> The dominion will be vast,
> and its prosperity will never end.
> He will reign on the throne of David
> and over his kingdom,
> to establish and sustain it
> with justice and righteousness from now on and forever.
> The zeal of the Lord of Armies will accomplish this.
>
> Isaiah 9:6–7 (CSB)

The kingship of God's domain has been given to Jesus, the Messiah.[5] Wherever Jesus rules, good triumphs over evil. He is wise, powerful, compassionate,

---

[4]John 18:36.
[5]Hebrews 1:2.

and peaceable. His domain is prosperous and stable. He governs with justice and righteousness. That sounds like a great place to live. I'd like to see it here on earth now.

What is the scope of his Kingdom?

> The Lord has established his throne in heaven,
> and his kingdom rules over all.
>
> Psalm 103:19 (CSB)

Heaven and earth are God's creation, so he is the owner of all. The domain of his kingdom includes everyone and all of the physical universe, including my backyard.

> Thy kingdom come, Thy will be done in earth, as it is in heaven.
>
> Matthew 6:10 (KJV)

Like Christians around the world, I pray the Lord's Prayer. I hope Jesus will return soon, so righteousness will be done in this world. However, the spiritual dimension of the Kingdom of Heaven means it is more than just Jesus taking over Planet Earth. Can I live in his Kingdom now, while I'm here on earth?

The discourses of Jesus

The Gospel of Matthew has five extensive passages called *discourses*. In them, Jesus taught about the Kingdom of Heaven.[6] Each discourse answers a question.

- What is the Kingdom of Heaven lifestyle? (5:1–7:29)

- What is the mission of disciples? (10:1–42)

- What is the Kingdom of Heaven like? (13:1–52)

- Who is the greatest in the Kingdom of Heaven? (18:1–35)

- What will be the signs of Jesus' coming as king? (24:1–25:46)

The answers show me how to live the Kingdom lifestyle now, help me fulfill the mission God has for me, give me understanding of the Kingdom, show me how to live a life pleasing to God, and prepare me for Jesus' coming.

Others may explain how the discourses fit into Matthew as a whole. They may analyze relationships among various parallel gospel accounts in Matthew, Mark, and Luke (the Synoptic Problem). They may discuss other controversies among Bible scholars. The focus here is personal application of the discourses of Jesus in Matthew.

---

[6]Matthew used the phrase the *Kingdom of Heaven* and Mark, Luke, and John used the phrase the *Kingdom of God*. The contexts of such passages indicate these phrases mean the same thing.

Outline

When I was a kid, my teachers taught me how to read an outline and how to make one. The levels were indented and each level had its own style of numbering. When I'm studying a book, I like to find the author's topics and thought patterns and then make an outline. It helps me remember what the author said and lets me know what to expect as I read each section.

Bible commentators often have different outlines of the discourses which reflect their differing interpretations. Some divisions between sections are obvious and some are ambiguous. The outline below is my opinion.[7]

The first level of my outline consists of the five discourses of Jesus. Matthew explained the setting before each discourse. The second level of the outline reflects major themes, and the third level is based on language patterns and literary structure.

I. Living in the Kingdom

    A. Citizens of the Kingdom

        1. Beatitudes 5:1–12

        2. Salt 5:13

        3. Light 5:14–16

    B. Law in the Kingdom

        1. Law fulfilled 5:17–20

        2. Murder 5:21–26

        3. Adultery 5:27–30

        4. Divorce 5:31–32

        5. Oaths 5:33–37

        6. Revenge 5:38–42

        7. Enemies 5:43–48

    C. Religion in the Kingdom

        1. Righteousness in public 6:1

        2. When you give to the poor 6:2–4

        3. When you pray 6:5–15

        4. When you fast 6:16–18

    D. Priorities in the Kingdom

        1. Do not serve money 6:19–24

---

[7]The outline here differs from the outline embedded in the *Christian Standard Bible*, which is the primary translation used by this book. Quoted passages may have paragraphs according to my outline.

III. The Kingdom is like...

    A. Why parables? 13:1–3,10–17,34–35

    B. Parables of the Kingdom

        1. A sower 13:3–9,18–23

        2. Wheat and tares 13:24–30,36–43

        3. A mustard seed 13:31–32

        4. Yeast 13:33

        5. Treasure 13:44

        6. A pearl 13:45–46

        7. A net 13:47–50

    C. Treasures new and old 13:51–52

IV. Greatest in the Kingdom

    A. Who is the greatest? 18:1–4

    B. Protect a child

        1. Welcome 18:5

        2. Do not cause to stumble 18:6–9

        3. Do not despise 18:10–11

        4. The lost sheep 18:12–14

    C. Reconcile with your brother

        1. Reconcile 18:15–17

        2. Binding and loosing 18:18

        3. In agreement 18:19–20

    D. Forgive your brother

        1. How many times? 18:21–22

        2. The unmerciful servant 18:23–35

V. The coming of the king

    A. Before his coming

        1. Birth pains 24:1–8

        2. Endure 24:9–13

        3. The gospel preached 24:14

        4. Flee 24:15–22

    B. His coming

        1. Not like false messiahs 24:23–28

       2. In the sky 24:29–31

C. When is he coming?

       1. A fig tree 24:32–35
       2. The days of Noah 24:36–42
       3. A homeowner 24:43–44
       4. Stewards 24:45–51
       5. Virgins 25:1–13

D. After his coming

       1. Talents 25:14–30
       2. Sheep and goats 25:31–46

Part I

Living in the Kingdom

2

Citizens of the Kingdom

Only the call and the promise, for the sake of which [the disciples] are ready to suffer poverty and renunciation, can justify the beatitudes.

Dietrich Bonhoeffer[1]

It seems odd that Jesus called his disciples *blessed* even though they would face poverty, rejection, and persecution. The Beatitudes make sense only to those who experience the call of Jesus and the promise of citizenship in the Kingdom of Heaven.

I became a citizen of the United States when I was born here. Some are citizens because their parents are citizens. Others choose to become citizens by naturalization. Citizenship has certain civic responsibilities and benefits. For example, I must pay taxes, and I get to vote in elections.

Citizenship in the Kingdom of Heaven also has responsibilities and benefits. Persecution may come because I am following the call of Jesus. Remolding my heart may be necessary. But Jesus promised eternal benefits.

This part's discourse is called the *Sermon on the Mount*, because Jesus sat on a hillside. In the Jewish culture of the time, it was customary for a teacher to be seated. Jesus spoke directly to the disciples who were up front with the crowd further back listening.

People chase after many lifestyles today. Lifestyles are marked by where one lives, where one shops, and how one spends time. People might pursue an urban lifestyle or country living. They buy clothes, cars, and other status symbols to advertise their lifestyle. They fill up their time with hobbies and entertainment to identify with their social group. What is the Kingdom of Heaven lifestyle? Jesus gave the answer in this discourse.

This chapter discusses the Beatitudes and the parables of salt and light. These passages present some of the responsibilities and benefits of citizenship in the Kingdom of Heaven.

---

[1]Bonhoeffer, p. 118.

11

Beatitudes

When I interviewed for a new job, I wanted to know all about the benefits. Where was the reserved parking? What were the employee discounts? What was the health insurance? What was the retirement plan? If I am going to be a disciple of Jesus, I want to know about the benefits, too.

This passage is called the *Beatitudes*, because it consists of a series of blessings.

Matthew 5:1–12 (KJV)[2]

---

1 And seeing the multitudes, he went up into a mountain: and when he was set, his disciples came unto him: 2 And he opened his mouth, and taught them, saying,

> 3 Blessed are the poor in spirit: for theirs is the kingdom of heaven.
> 4 Blessed are they that mourn: for they shall be comforted.
> 5 Blessed are the meek: for they shall inherit the earth.
> 6 Blessed are they which do hunger and thirst after righteousness: for they shall be filled.
> 7 Blessed are the merciful: for they shall obtain mercy.
> 8 Blessed are the pure in heart: for they shall see God.
> 9 Blessed are the peacemakers: for they shall be called the children of God.
> 10 Blessed are they which are persecuted for righteousness' sake: for theirs is the kingdom of heaven.

11 Blessed are ye, when men shall revile you, and persecute you, and shall say all manner of evil against you falsely, for my sake. 12 Rejoice, and be exceeding glad: for great is your reward in heaven: for so persecuted they the prophets which were before you.

The Greek word for *blessed*[3] is difficult to translate. The word *happy*, used by some translations, is too superficial, implying only an emotional state. The United Bible Societies suggests, "a harmonious relationship in which one party, usually the superior, does good to the other."[4]

Verse 3 and verse 10 delimit the beginning and end of the poetry by giving the same blessing in both verses, "theirs is the Kingdom of Heaven." This implies the verses in between are also about the Kingdom of Heaven. There are many other benefits to living in the Kingdom in addition to having the

---

[2]Luke 6:20–23 is a parallel passage.
[3]The Greek word *makarios* (*Strong's* No. 3107).
[4]United Bible Societies, *Translator Handbook, s.v.* Matthew 5:3–12.

Kingdom, as explained in the rest of the Beatitudes. This passage is completed by a final blessing in prose, elaborating on persecution.

Blessed are the poor in spirit. Virgia was surprised in her later years when she learned she had lived below the government's poverty line for most of her life. But she never felt poor, because God always provided for her. When you have the Kingdom of Heaven, you don't feel poor, no matter what level of financial resources you happen to have.

This beatitude promises the Kingdom of Heaven to the poor in spirit. They are blessed.

> Listen, my dear brothers and sisters: Didn't God choose the poor in this world to be rich in faith and heirs of the kingdom that he has promised to those who love him?
>
> James 2:5 (CSB)

A homeless guy lived in the woods next to my church for many years. The church staff got to know him. Then in the middle of a Sunday service, I saw him at the back of the church, kneeling on the floor, praying. I found out later he had received the Holy Spirit into his life.

God operates differently than the world. The Kingdom belongs to the poor in spirit. He calls ordinary people, especially from the lowest strata of society. They understand his grace and they respond in faith. The church in Corinth is an example where the gospel attracted the poor.

> Brothers and sisters, consider your calling: Not many were wise from a human perspective, not many powerful, not many of noble birth. Instead, God has chosen what is foolish in the world to shame the wise, and God has chosen what is weak in the world to shame the strong. God has chosen what is insignificant and despised in the world—what is viewed as nothing—to bring to nothing what is viewed as something, so that no one may boast in his presence.
>
> 1 Corinthians 1:26–29 (CSB)

The Christians in Corinth were not from the upper echelons of society. They were not intellectuals, and they were not politically powerful, rich, or famous. The Kingdom message was welcomed by the poor, the oppressed, and the anonymous. The poor often receive the gospel of the Kingdom of Heaven more easily than those who are not.[5]

The Kingdom message is not exclusive. Anyone can receive Jesus by faith. However, those who have honor, power, fame, and riches have obstacles to faith. Intellectuals try to enter the Kingdom by reasoning about God. The politically powerful try to enter the Kingdom by achieving great things. The rich or famous think they deserve to enter the Kingdom, because everyone honors them. None of these things gain entrance to the Kingdom.

The benefits of having the Kingdom are better than being rich or famous.

---

[5] 19:23–26.

For the kingdom of God is not eating and drinking, but righteousness, peace, and joy in the Holy Spirit.

> Romans 14:17 (CSB)

The Kingdom is not about living under rules and regulations, but rather a
life filled with righteousness, peace, and joy. Most of the Beatitudes use future
tense, but *theirs is the kingdom* is present tense. The poor in spirit are citizens of
the Kingdom now.

The benefit of being poor in spirit is having the Kingdom of Heaven. The
poor in spirit are blessed because the Kingdom of Heaven belongs to them,
which is much more valuable than material possessions. Citizenship in the
Kingdom comes with great benefits.

Blessed are they that mourn. My uncle's funeral was a time for mourning,
because we all will miss him. The funeral was also a celebration of his life and
the wonderful influence he had been on others. We all knew he was in the
arms of his Savior. The Kingdom of Heaven offers hope that reaches beyond
the grave. The hope of eternal life comforts Christians whose believing loved
ones have died. God's grace provides true comfort.

Mourning is occasioned by loss. The opposite of a loss is a gift. Comfort
from God is his gift to citizens of the Kingdom. They are blessed.

> When Jesus arrived, he found that Lazarus had already been in the
> tomb four days...
>
> When Jesus saw [Mary] crying, and the Jews who had come
> with her crying, he was deeply moved in his spirit and troubled.
> "Where have you put him?" he asked.
> "Lord," they told him, "come and see."
> Jesus wept.
>
> John 11:17,33–35 (CSB)

Jesus mourned with Mary and Martha when he arrived at the tomb of
Lazarus, even though he knew he would raise his friend from the dead in a
few minutes. He shared their grief.

We mourn when a loved one dies. We also mourn when someone else's
loved one dies. Sometimes we mourn over a circumstance or other loss. Sometimes death is the completion of a full life. Sometimes victims die prematurely,
victims of sickness, accidents, foolishness, or sin. Sickness and accidents happen because we are all human. Some accidents are the result of foolish choices.
A person in a sinful lifestyle may die as a result, or a person may die as the innocent victim of someone else's sin. These premature deaths are all tragedies.
We grieve over them.

> Rejoice with those who rejoice; weep with those who weep.
>
> Romans 12:15 (CSB)

A neighborhood watch volunteer in Florida shot a young man who was beating him.[6] People having dinner in a London restaurant were killed by terrorists with knives.[7] A young woman was run over by a car at a political demonstration in Virginia.[8] A child was killed by a stray bullet in Chicago.[9] The news is full of reports of mothers mourning the deaths of their children.

As just one person, I have a limited capacity for mourning, so I carefully select news stories I mourn over. I mourn over the situations the Holy Spirit chooses for me, mostly in daily life and sometimes around the world. This old world is so sinful that there are multitudes of suffering people to mourn with. But locally, I can mourn with acquaintances and be an instrument of God's comforting power.

> The Spirit of the Lord God is on me,
> because the Lord has anointed me
> to bring good news to the poor.
> He has sent me to heal the brokenhearted…
> to comfort all who mourn,
> to provide for those who mourn in Zion;
> to give them a crown of beauty instead of ashes,
> festive oil instead of mourning,
> and splendid clothes instead of despair.
>
> Isaiah 61:1–3 (CSB)

Jesus promised comfort for grieving disciples. Jesus' mission, foretold by Isaiah, included healing broken hearts and comforting those who mourn. In ancient times, ashes on the head and clothes were an outward sign of mourning, but oil in the hair was a sign of good grooming. Isaiah prophesied the Messiah will bring such complete comfort that outward signs of joy will replace ashes, lack of grooming, and dirty clothes.

When I mourn over a situation, I pray the Lord's grace will turn the situation around and bring about good from tragedy. For example, when Judah was carried into captivity by the Babylonians, they wept over the loss of their homeland and their place of worship.[10] In due course, God's grace turned that situation around and restored a remnant to their land.

I have mourned the deaths of parents, grandparents, aunts, uncles, cousins, and dear friends. Attending a funeral may provide some closure, but I still feel

---

[6]"The Trayvon Martin case: A timeline," *The Week*, July 17, 2012. Available at http://theweek.com/articles/476855/trayvon-martin-case-timeline (Current March 1, 2019).

[7]"London Bridge terror: Seven killed in van and knife attack, three attackers shot dead," *Sky News*, June 4, 2017. Available at https://news.sky.com/story/knife-attack-after-car-mounts-pavement-in-london-reports-10903580 (Current March 1, 2019).

[8]"Deadly car attack, violent clashes in Charlottesville: What we know now," *USA Today*, August 13, 2017. Available at https://www.usatoday.com/story/news/nation/2017/08/13/charlottesville-protests-what-we-know-now/562911001/ (Current March 1, 2019).

[9]Katherine Rosenberg-Douglas, Jason Meisner, and Gregory Pratt, "Third child dies from a shooting in Chicago in just two days," *Chicago Tribune*, February 15, 2017. http://www.chicagotribune.com/news/local/breaking/ct-children-shot-chicago-20170215-story.html (Current March 1, 2019).

[10]Psalm 137:1–6.

each loss. The stories of their lives are precious. Listing reasons for a loss does not provide much comfort, because the mind can hardly touch the hurting soul. As a citizen of the Kingdom, when I mourn, God comforts deep down in my soul beyond explanation, beyond reason, and then I can share God's comfort with others.

Blessed are the meek. Why would any guy want to be meek? I thought men are supposed to be strong, proud, and in charge of the situation. Then I read the Bible. Jesus said the meek will inherit the land. Maybe I need to adjust my idea of manliness. This beatitude promises an inheritance to the meek.

The word *meek*[11] is associated with humility, gentleness, and powerlessness. The *Christian Standard Bible* prefers *humble* instead of the King James Version's *meek*. The powerless tend to have a gentle, humble demeanor due to their situation. Jesus is my model of a meek attitude.

> Adopt the same attitude as that of Christ Jesus,
> who, existing in the form of God,
> did not consider equality with God
> as something to be exploited.
> Instead he emptied himself
> by assuming the form of a servant,
> taking on the likeness of humanity.
> And when he had come as a man,
> he humbled himself by becoming obedient
> to the point of death—
> even to death on a cross.
>
> Philippians 2:5–8 (CSB)

Jesus was humble even though he was God. He became a human being and was so obedient he willingly went to the cross.

There are several components of meekness. I will be gentle and humble. I will not strive for the praise of men. I will have confidence in who I am, knowing God loves me and will bring justice for me when I need it. I will respect others, and will be willing to associate with all kinds of people.[12]

Meek does not mean low self-esteem. It means having high esteem for everyone else.[13] *Meek* does not mean weak. It takes strength of character to resist evil.[14]

The meek are guaranteed an inheritance.

> But the meek shall inherit the earth; and shall delight themselves in the abundance of peace.
>
> Psalm 37:11 (KJV)

---

[11] The Greek word *praupathia* (*Strong's* No. 4239).
[12] Romans 12:16.
[13] 1 Peter 2:17.
[14] Ephesians 6:11–13.

Angie's grandfather was a farmer, so her father and his sister inherited the family's homestead. Because they could not farm it themselves, a neighbor rented the land. Society in ancient times was based on agriculture. Land was the most important inheritance passed from generation to generation.

In ancient Israel, the *meek* referred to the peasants who worked the land. They were the humble powerless stratum of society. Jesus referred to Psalm 37:11 when he said, "Blessed are the meek: for they shall inherit the earth." When Jesus mentioned Psalm 37, the entire psalm was brought to mind by his listeners. Here are some selected verses from that psalm.

> 1 Do not be agitated by evildoers;
> do not envy those who do wrong...
> 3 Trust in the Lord and do what is good;
> dwell in the land and live securely.
> 4 Take delight in the Lord,
> and he will give you your heart's desires...
> 9 For evildoers will be destroyed,
> but those who put their hope in the Lord
> will inherit the land...
> 11 But the humble will inherit the land
> and will enjoy abundant prosperity...
> 22 Those who are blessed by the Lord will inherit the land,
> but those cursed by him will be destroyed...
> 27 Turn away from evil, do what is good,
> and settle permanently...
> 29 The righteous will inherit the land
> and dwell in it permanently...
>
> Psalm 37:1–40 (CSB)

Psalm 37 lists many godly qualities associated with the phrases *inherit the land* or *dwell in the land*. The meek trust in the Lord. They delight in the Lord. They hope in the Lord. They are humble. They are blessed by the Lord. They do good. They are righteous. As a result, they will have the land as a permanent possession and dwell there. Whenever there is conflict with evil men, the Lord will give them justice.

As citizens of the Kingdom of Heaven, we have a share in an inheritance in Jesus' Kingdom.

> Giving thanks to the Father, who has enabled you to share in the saints' inheritance in the light. He has rescued us from the domain of darkness and transferred us into the kingdom of the Son he loves.
>
> Colossians 1:12–13 (CSB)

Developing a meek attitude like Jesus has, and trusting in the Lord like Psalm 37 recommends is the way to live. Then I will have an inheritance as a citizen in the Kingdom of Heaven. This sounds much better than inheriting physical land, because I'm not very good at farming.

Blessed are they which do hunger and thirst after righteousness. I love bread, all kinds of bread: white bread, whole wheat, pumpernickel, rye bread, corn bread, pita bread, and on and on. I'll put butter on it or jelly or maybe just eat it plain. I like it for sandwiches or even dessert. But pumpernickel won't satisfy my hunger for righteousness.

This beatitude promises satisfaction to those who earnestly desire righteousness. They are blessed.

If I am uncomfortable, I'll try to fix my surroundings. If it is too hot, I'll push the thermostat down. If I see dust balls on the floor, I'll get out the vacuum cleaner. My neighbor was a drummer in a band. He practiced almost every afternoon. I closed my windows, but that wasn't enough. Sometimes it's hard to fix my surroundings.

Those who hunger for righteousness can recognize evil. They can discern between righteousness and unrighteousness. There is a famine of righteousness in this world. Evil abounds. I often get disgusted with the lack of righteousness around me. I long for Christ's righteous reign on the earth. He will fix my surroundings.

> For the kingdom of God is not eating and drinking, but righteousness, peace, and joy in the Holy Spirit.
>
> Romans 14:17 (CSB)

The Kingdom of Heaven is about internal qualities like righteousness. The promise of this beatitude is to be filled with God's righteousness. However, this has nothing to do with my environment. It is all about his righteousness in me.

What kind of bread will satisfy my hunger for righteousness? Toasted or plain? Sliced or a bun? Can I eat a "righteousness sandwich"?

> "I am the bread of life," Jesus told them. "No one who comes to me will ever be hungry, and no one who believes in me will ever be thirsty again."
>
> John 6:35 (CSB)

The "bread of life" will satisfy my hunger for righteousness. Jesus himself is that bread. The way to satisfy my hunger is to come to Jesus and believe in him. This means becoming his disciple, one hundred percent. In return, Jesus promised eternal life.[15]

A kitchen sink is an amazing invention. Hot and cold water are available at the turn of a knob. It is so convenient. Can my thirst for righteousness be satisfied at the kitchen sink?

> But whoever drinks from the water that I will give him will never get thirsty again. In fact, the water I will give him will become a well of water springing up in him for eternal life.
>
> John 4:14 (CSB)

---

[15]John 6:51.

18

Jesus met a Samaritan woman at Jacob's well. She thought he was promising her a kitchen sink. Instead, he offered her water that gives eternal life. What is this spring of water?

> On the last and most important day of the festival, Jesus stood up and cried out, "If anyone is thirsty, let him come to me and drink. The one who believes in me, as the Scripture has said, will have streams of living water flow from deep within him." He said this about the Spirit. Those who believed in Jesus were going to receive the Spirit, for the Spirit had not yet been given because Jesus had not yet been glorified.
>
> John 7:37–39 (CSB)

Deep in the Ocala National Forest, thirteen million gallons of water per day are gushing from Juniper Springs, filling a swimming hole and a creek. If one is thirsty, there is plenty of clean cool water to drink.

Jesus promised a spring of living water from deep within each believer. John explained the Holy Spirit is the living water that will satisfy my thirst for righteousness.

The Holy Spirit on the inside results in good works in action. Paul advised Timothy to pursue righteousness and godly character.

> But you, man of God, flee from these [evil] things, and pursue righteousness, godliness, faith, love, endurance, and gentleness.
>
> 1 Timothy 6:11 (CSB)

After a long winter in storage outside, my lawn mower wouldn't run. It was dirty inside and out from last summer. I had to take it to the shop for an overhaul. When I look inside at my natural self, I see a bitter cynical arrogant person. My character needs an overhaul, too.

Hunger and thirst for God's righteousness didn't stop when I first believed. I am pursuing his righteousness day by day. The natural person is gradually changing into godly qualities.[16] Righteous works follow from having God's righteousness inside of me.

Blessed are the merciful. As the truck was unloaded at our new home, we saw one piece of broken furniture after another. About half of our furniture was ruined by an accident the truck had on the way. We had to forgive the driver.

This beatitude promises mercy for those who extend mercy to others. They are blessed.

Mercy is when forgiveness and compassion abound. I can forgive others in two situations: (1) I am the victim of someone's sin; and (2) someone acciden-

---

[16]Ephesians 4:22–24.

19

tally does something that hurts me. The root of sin is rebellion. If a person is not rebelling against the Lord, he can still make a mistake or have an accident.[17]

> And we exhort you, brothers and sisters: warn those who are idle, comfort the discouraged, help the weak, be patient with everyone. See to it that no one repays evil for evil to anyone, but always pursue what is good for one another and for all.
>
> 1 Thessalonians 5:14–15 (CSB)

Sometimes a brother is accident-prone. He might be immature. He might be in a hurry. He might be weak. He might be clumsy. If I'm nearby, I might get hurt. Accidents happen.

I will help my brother, even at the risk of an accident. If I get hurt, I must forgive. My priority is to do what is good for others and to be patient with their weaknesses, because God forgives my weaknesses.[18]

> And be kind and compassionate to one another, forgiving one another, just as God also forgave you in Christ.
>
> Ephesians 4:32 (CSB)

When I began to make career choices, I gravitated toward engineering. My grandfather was an engineer. My father was an engineer, and I became an engineer. A child imitates his parents.

A citizen of the Kingdom is merciful, because he is imitating his heavenly Father. God was merciful to me when he forgave my sin. When I forgive someone, I then feel compassionate toward him and react with kindness whenever needed. God feels the same way toward me.

> But God, who is rich in mercy, because of his great love that he had for us, made us alive with Christ even though we were dead in trespasses. You are saved by grace!
>
> Ephesians 2:4–5 (CSB)

Merciful describes God's character. His mercy is motivated by his love for mankind. He demonstrated his mercy toward rebellious Israel over and over.[19] He was merciful during the Exodus as they trekked across the Sinai. He was merciful when they worshiped idols. He was merciful even through the Babylonian captivity.

He has shown the same mercy to me. Because of his mercy, he saved me through the death and resurrection of Jesus.[20] I will be merciful to others, because I need God's mercy over my life.

---

[17]Jesus also taught about forgiving offenses later in the Sermon on the Mount (6:14–15) and in the discourse on who is greatest (18:21–35).

[18]Romans 15:1–2.

[19]Isaiah 30:18.

[20]1 Peter 1:3.

Blessed are the pure in heart. I own a shirt made of 100 percent pure cotton. No man-made fibers are mixed in the fabric, no nylon, no rayon, no polyester, no elastane. My shirt has all the benefits of pure cotton.

This beatitude promises intimacy with God to those with a pure heart. They are blessed.

> Now the goal of our instruction is love that comes from a pure heart, a good conscience, and a sincere faith.
>
> 1 Timothy 1:5 (CSB)

Pure means one type of substance without mixture with something else. Twenty-four karat gold is pure gold. Other cheaper metals are not mixed in.

The *heart* in biblical culture meant the innermost core of a person. When God created mankind, he made his image to be the core of each person.[21] A pure heart is God's image inside me with no contamination from sin in any area.

True purity is in the heart rather than external ritual, because out of the heart flows thoughts of the mind, feelings, and emotions, and decisions of the will. From these flow words and behavior. The impure heart is the source of sinful actions.[22] A pure heart is the source of self-sacrificing love.

> How can a young man keep his way pure?
> By keeping your word.
>
> Psalm 119:9 (CSB)

The ground was mostly clay. When it rained, my bare yard became thick mud. I had to wear rubber boots whenever I did yard work. When I finished I had to get out the hose to wash the mud off my boots.

Living among people in this fallen world means I often get mud on the boots of my soul. There is much impurity in society. Advertising, TV shows, the news, and conversations with worldly friends all display the impurity of mankind. A cutting word, a petty theft, a little white lie, or some outrageous selfishness is enough to make me feel defiled. A few minutes of prayer and worship washes my soul.

How can a person get a pure heart? Purity before God is not achieved by fulfilling some ritual washing. It is not gained by fulfilling some religious duty. Purity is the result of the cleansing action of the Holy Spirit. Obeying the Word of God keeps my mud from splattering on those around me.[23]

What are the benefits of a pure heart?

> Who may ascend the mountain of the Lord?
> Who may stand in his holy place?
> The one who has clean hands and a pure heart,
> who has not appealed to what is false,

---

[21] Genesis 1:27.
[22] Mark 7:20–23.
[23] 1 Peter 1:22.

and who has not sworn deceitfully.
He will receive blessing from the Lord,
and righteousness from the God of his salvation.

Psalm 24:3–5 (CSB)

In biblical times, pilgrims went to Jerusalem to worship several times each year. I can imagine the effort to walk uphill toward the city and its temple. Who could rightfully go to the hill where the temple in Jerusalem was located?—The pure in heart. Who could stand in the place of God's presence?—The pure in heart.

The blessing of a pure heart is intimacy with God. When my heart is pure, then spiritual intimacy with God is easy, because there is no sin blocking fellowship, relationship, and communication with him.

Today, intimacy with God is not limited to Jerusalem, to special worship services, or to special places like cathedrals. It can happen in the flow of daily life, walking down the hall at work, talking with someone, driving in traffic, writing an email, and on and on.

Blessed are the peacemakers. The men in the family seemed to always be at war with each other. Brothers, in-laws, and cousins always seemed to take offense at something. Aunt Virgia had the gift of peacemaking. She was able to reconcile even the most argumentative.

The Hebrew word for *peace*[24] implies complete well-being. When Jesus stated this beatitude, his audience thought of well-being. Peace is not just the absence of war. Peace is found in relationships. There is peace with oneself, with one's neighbor, among organizations, among nations, with God, and even with that irritating cousin.

This beatitude promises a place in God's family to those who are peacemakers. They are blessed.

> Don't worry about anything, but in everything, through prayer and petition with thanksgiving, present your requests to God. And the peace of God, which surpasses all understanding, will guard your hearts and minds in Christ Jesus.
>
> Philippians 4:6–7 (CSB)

When I worry about something, it goes around and around in my mind. "Maybe this will work. Maybe that will happen." All the possible scenarios fill up my thoughts. But when I talk to God about my problem, he lets me know he is in control. Then his peace invades my soul.

To be a peacemaker, I must first have peace myself. Salvation opens the way for the peace of God to flood in. Peace is a fruit of the Spirit.[25] I don't need to be anxious. I am confident in my relationship with God. When there is peace inside, then I am able to influence those around me, to be a peacemaker, instead of letting strife take over.

---

[24]The Hebrew word *shalom* (*Strong's* No. 7965).
[25]Galatians 5:22.

Better a dry crust with peace
than a house full of feasting with strife.

Proverbs 17:1 (CSB)

Living in peace is more important than prosperity with strife. Too often people get in arguments over a few dollars. Being at war prevents one from enjoying what one has.

When people have been at war, stopping the war is the first step. Peacemakers go in the middle of warring combatants. Peacemakers are willing to risk relationships with each side. Healing wounds is another step, which entails forgiving the other side. In most wars, there is plenty of blame to go around. Forgiveness and confession are God's way to overcome sin in relationships. Afterward, more steps build trust that leads to peace and well-being. A peacemaker facilitates this process.

I am not in a position to influence world peace. I can't resolve the Arab-Israeli conflict. I can't stop military aggression. However, I can influence the people around me,[26] because I know the source of peace, the Prince of Peace. He makes peace grow from the inside out. Being called sons of God implies when others see peacemakers at work, they will recognize peacemakers are like their Father.

Blessed are they which are persecuted for righteousness' sake. Whenever her brother-in-law came to visit, my friend could count on facing his subtle style of persecution, full of barbs, innuendo, and snide remarks. Even though he was once a passionate believer himself, he would probe the Christians in the family, ready to pounce on any compromise or weakness.

The last two Beatitudes are for those who are persecuted. The first blessing is the Kingdom of Heaven. The second blessing is a great reward waiting in heaven just like the reward prepared for the prophets of old. Who are the persecutors? Why do they persecute Christians?

This is the judgment: The light has come into the world, and people loved darkness rather than the light because their deeds were evil. For everyone who does evil hates the light and avoids it, so that his deeds may not be exposed.

John 3:19–20 (CSB)

My supervisor told me to charge a contract project on my time card, even though I was working on an overhead task. Falsifying a time card is a criminal offense. The management above me was trying to cover up their misuse of project funds. I suspect my refusal limited my potential advancement in that company.

In the world, people hate righteousness because they do evil things. The motive of the persecutor is often not apparent at first, because it is cloaked in

---

[26]Romans 12:18.

23

some external offense. Eventually, motives are revealed. This beatitude says there is a blessing for the victim when there is hostility toward righteousness.

Living in righteousness is more important than avoiding conflict. Those living in sin do not like to be near those living in righteousness, so persecution naturally follows.

> But if anyone suffers as a Christian, let him not be ashamed but let him glorify God in having that name.
>
> 1 Peter 4:16 (CSB)

Jesus said disciples will be persecuted, not only for righteousness, but also because of him. He is the ultimate righteous one. Evil people living in darkness hate the Christ. They often espouse atheism, wishing God's justice would just go away. Someone who openly follows Jesus is an easy target for those who want to vent their hatred toward Jesus. When evil people have power, they use it to slander those who identify with Jesus.

> Conduct yourselves honorably among the Gentiles, so that when they slander you as evildoers, they will observe your good works and will glorify God on the day he visits.
>
> 1 Peter 2:12 (CSB)

False accusation is another tactic of those who hate righteousness and hate Jesus. When all is in the sunshine, false accusations are obvious for what they are. Most of the time, when accusations are shown to be false, they lose their power. However, sometimes evil people will cling to falsehood even when evidence confirms the truth. They did that to Jesus. Truth in all of life is part of Kingdom living.[27]

Why are the persecuted blessed? Why should they rejoice? First, the Kingdom belongs to them, present tense. Second, *great is your reward in heaven* means future possession but present ownership.

> For our momentary light affliction is producing for us an absolutely incomparable eternal weight of glory. So we do not focus on what is seen, but on what is unseen. For what is seen is temporary, but what is unseen is eternal.
>
> 2 Corinthians 4:17–18 (CSB)

When Rachel's college literature class discussed a culture that practiced human sacrifice, she argued God's moral law is absolute, so human sacrifice is murder. Everyone in the class attacked her, "How can you say that about another culture?" As she left class, she wondered whether she had any friends left in that class, but she knew she had the Kingdom of Heaven.

Paul told the Corinthians the future reward far outweighs life's temporary hardships. Like the poor in spirit, the Kingdom belongs to the persecuted right

---

[27]Ephesians 4:25; 5:8–10.

now. Persecution is never pleasant, but even during a bad experience, those persecuted for righteousness are blessed by God at that very moment, as well as in the future.

> Rejoice as you share in the sufferings of Christ, so that you may also rejoice with great joy when his glory is revealed.
>
> 1 Peter 4:13 (CSB)

When Becky was ten years old, her ballet teacher demonstrated the *pas de chat*. When she tried to imitate her teacher, it was awkward. Oops! She fell on the floor. She got up and kept trying. The teacher showed her how to move. She was ecstatic when she did it properly at a performance.

When I try to imitate Jesus, it's awkward. I may fail and others may criticize me, but I'll keep trying. I know the truth of God's love and I recognize the lies of the opposition. I may have to suffer like he did, but I'll rejoice when he returns in glory.

Blessed are citizens of the Kingdom. The Beatitudes characterize the citizens of the Kingdom. They are poor in spirit. They mourn with the grieving. They are humble and gentle. They desire righteousness. They extend forgiveness. They have pure hearts. They reconcile warring parties. They are abused, insulted, and falsely accused by the world. They are identified by their character qualities, by the depth of their relationship with God, and by the reaction of the world to their lives.

There are many benefits of living the lifestyle of the Beatitudes. Citizens have the Kingdom of Heaven. They shall be comforted. They shall receive an inheritance. They shall be filled with righteousness. They shall obtain mercy. They shall see God. They shall be called the children of God. They have the Kingdom of Heaven (again). They have joy and a great reward in heaven. The citizens of the Kingdom are blessed.

Salt

I like fried eggs and bacon for breakfast. The bacon is always cured with salt, and I like salt and pepper on my eggs. Breakfast just wouldn't be the same if we didn't have salt.

Matthew 5:13 (CSB)

---

13 You are the salt of the earth. But if the salt should lose its taste, how can it be made salty? It's no longer good for anything but to be thrown out and trampled under people's feet.

In ancient times, every family understood salt is necessary for good health. Salt adds flavor to food and can prevent food from spoiling. Regions without salt engaged in expensive trade over long distances to get it.

Is bland food eaten without salt?
Is there flavor in an egg white?

Job 6:6 (CSB)

Like today, salt was important in ancient times for adding flavor to food.[28]
Job couldn't imagine eating something as bland as an egg white without salt.

I can add flavor to life around me, like salt. A smile, a kind word, or a
courtesy can brighten someone's day. I've adopted the Southern custom of
greeting strangers I pass on the sidewalk or in the grocery store aisle. There are
many small ways to make the lives of others more interesting.

Let your speech always be gracious, seasoned with salt, so that you
may know how you should answer each person.

Colossians 4:6 (CSB)

As I walked into the room, I could hear my coworker swearing about something, punctuating every other sentence with some obscenity. When he saw
me, he said, "Oh, excuse me."

The presence of a Christian sometimes acts like disinfectant on the speech
of others, like salt. I'm not offended when worldly people talk like worldly
people. Even though I don't like it, I don't make a scene when the talk around
me profanes the Lord's name or is filthy. But I try to make my conversation
clean, clear, and courteous.

In ancient times, salt was not refined to be pure sodium chloride, like we
have today. So, the sodium chloride itself might get leeched out, leaving a
worthless residue. Those who go astray from the faith are like that residue.

[False teachers] have gone astray by abandoning the straight path
and have followed the path of Balaam, the son of Bosor, who loved
the wages of wickedness.

2 Peter 2:15 (CSB)

A friend who grew up in church was a committed believer into her twen-
ties. However, she was wounded by a church scandal and abandoned Christian fellowship. Later, it seemed secular social-justice activism replaced following Jesus. Her life lost the flavor of the Kingdom.

A citizen of the Kingdom, like salt, can have a positive influence on our
culture, can flavor life for others, and can disinfect conversations. But if a person goes astray, like the false teachers Peter warned about, the life of God gets
leeched out leaving a worthless lifestyle.

My life as a follower of Jesus contributes to the health of our culture. Some
Christians participate in public aspects of culture, such as media, politics, and
arts. Most of us don't affect these public spheres much, but I can influence the
workplaces, schools, and community groups around me.

---

[28]Job asked these rhetorical questions when describing the depth of his grief.

Light

The city was draped over some rolling hills next to the railroad tracks. The dairy plant was situated at the tracks. The best houses in town were a short uphill walk. A block from the tracks, Main Street went up to the county courthouse. From the railroad tracks, the lighted town was obvious.

Matthew 5:14–16 (CSB)

---

14 You are the light of the world. A city situated on a hill cannot be hidden. 15 No one lights a lamp and puts it under a basket, but rather on a lampstand, and it gives light for all who are in the house. 16 In the same way, let your light shine before others, so that they may see your good works and give glory to your Father in heaven.

In these verses, the light represents good works. John used light to represent Jesus himself.[29] These two analogies fit together, because the source of light in me comes from following Jesus.

Jerusalem is an example of a city situated on several hills.

The Lord is great and highly praised
in the city of our God.
His holy mountain, rising splendidly,
is the joy of the whole earth.

Psalm 48:1–2 (CSB)

Jerusalem is easily recognized from a distance. When the psalmist saw the city, he began praising the Lord, because it was the place God had chosen as the seat of his Kingdom. Like Jerusalem, good deeds by disciples are often obvious to the community.

Philanthropists usually want public recognition for their generosity, maybe a plaque or a building named after them. But a disciple's good deeds are not intended to make him feel honored. I don't do good deeds to become famous, but when I do them, God should get the glory while I remain almost anonymous.

For we are his workmanship, created in Christ Jesus for good works, which God prepared ahead of time for us to do.

Ephesians 2:10 (CSB)

I had been learning to play guitar for a few years when the neck of my guitar broke. The next Sunday, a guy at church said, "Ed, will this fit your guitar strap? The Holy Spirit told me to give this to you." He gave me a very fine guitar. I was the recipient of a good work. I've been telling people ever since how the Lord gave me my guitar.

---

[29] John 1:4–9 and John 8:12.

Following Jesus results in good deeds which cannot and should not be hidden. When people benefit from good deeds, they should praise God. Kingdom living results in thanksgiving to the Father in heaven. In our modern world, achieving this may mean the deed is public, but the doer is anonymous.[30]

Good deeds are the evidence of the gospel at work in my life. A small act of kindness can mean much to someone who is having a difficult day. For a follower of Jesus, acts of kindness are a way of life, light shining in the darkness.

Citizens of the Kingdom

Who are the citizens of the Kingdom of Heaven? Is having Christian parents an automatic ticket? What about Christian grandparents? Is becoming a church member enough? Where can I sign up?

> Jesus Christ, the faithful witness, the firstborn from the dead and the ruler of the kings of the earth.
> To him who loves us and has set us free from our sins by his blood, and made us a kingdom, priests to his God and Father—to him be glory and dominion forever and ever. Amen.
> Revelation 1:5–6 (CSB)

By dying on the cross, Jesus freed me from my sins. Consequently, I am a citizen of the Kingdom of Heaven. My citizenship has certain responsibilities and benefits. I must follow Jesus as a disciple, and he has promised me eternal life.[31] All who have been set free by Jesus are citizens of his Kingdom.

Beatitudes. The Beatitudes characterize the citizens of the Kingdom and the kind of relationship they have with God. Their hearts are in tune with their savior, and they have the Kingdom of Heaven.

Salt. Jesus compared the citizens of the Kingdom to salt. The community of faith functions like salt in society, bringing glory to God for their flavor and their disinfectant presence.

Light. Jesus also compared the good works of the citizens of the Kingdom to a city on a hill and a lighted lamp. The community of faith cannot be hidden. Their good works are obvious like a city on a hill. Their good works are appreciated even though they may be anonymous.

Citizens of the Kingdom. Citizenship in the Kingdom is available to all who will repent of their sin. Family heritage doesn't matter. Joining an organization doesn't matter. Citizens of the Kingdom of Heaven have a personal relationship with God and are following Jesus as his disciples.

---

[30] 6:3.
[31] John 3:16.

3

Law in the Kingdom

The only way of overcoming this legalism is by real obedience to Christ when he calls us to follow him; for in Jesus the law is at once fulfilled and canceled.

Dietrich Bonhoeffer[1]

Religious Jews in Jesus' time thought legalism was the way to please God. The rabbis had transformed the Old Testament Law into many precise rules which the Pharisees were careful to obey. They thought obeying the Law was the ideal way to live one's life.

What is the place of the Law in the Kingdom? Jesus illustrated the principles of the Kingdom by discussing familiar laws everyone knew.[2] Simple obedience to Jesus means just following him, which in turn, fulfills the Law.

Law fulfilled

There are many household items that have become obsolete over the years. My grandmother's house had an upright piano. My mother and her sisters gathered around it and sang for the rest of the family—live music at home! Later, recorded music became more common, such as 78s, 45s, LPs, 8 tracks, cassettes, CDs, iPods, MP3 players, smart phones, and now streaming. Stuff becomes obsolete, but God's Word will never be obsolete.

Matthew 5:17–20 (CSB)

---

17 Don't think that I came to abolish the Law or the Prophets. I did not come to abolish but to fulfill. 18 For truly I tell you, until heaven

---

[1]Bonhoeffer, p. 92.

[2]The outline groups the illustrations in 5:17–48, because each one begins with *You have heard,* or a similar phrase.

and earth pass away, not the smallest letter or one stroke of a letter will pass away from the law until all things are accomplished. 19 Therefore, whoever breaks one of the least of these commands and teaches others to do the same will be called least in the kingdom of heaven. But whoever does and teaches these commands will be called great in the kingdom of heaven. 20 For I tell you, unless your righteousness surpasses that of the scribes and Pharisees, you will never get into the kingdom of heaven.

The *Law* generally referred to the first five books of the Old Testament, written by Moses, called the *Torah*. The *Law and the Prophets* together referred to the entire Old Testament. The Christian community affirmed the New Testament canon is also the authoritative Word of God, so the above passage in Matthew can be applied to the whole Bible.

What does it mean to fulfill the Word of God?

> The scroll of the prophet Isaiah was given to [Jesus], and unrolling the scroll, he found the place where it was written:
>
> > The Spirit of the Lord is on me,
> > because he has anointed me
> > to preach good news to the poor.
> > He has sent me
> > to proclaim release to the captives
> > and recovery of sight to the blind,
> > to set free the oppressed,
> > to proclaim the year of the Lord's favor.
>
> He then rolled up the scroll, gave it back to the attendant, and sat down. And the eyes of everyone in the synagogue were fixed on him. He began by saying to them, "Today as you listen, this Scripture has been fulfilled."
>
> Luke 4:17–21 (CSB)

Jesus read from the book of Isaiah in the synagogue as usual. He was doing the things listed there, so the passage was fulfilled in him. Jesus has fulfilled, is fulfilling, and will fulfill the Word of God.

I also have a part in accomplishing what the Word says. Living in the Kingdom demonstrates the truth of the Bible, which will last forever.

> Lord, your word is forever;
> it is firmly fixed in heaven.
> Your faithfulness is for all generations;
> you established the earth, and it stands firm.
>
> Psalm 119:89–90 (CSB)

There are many expressions whose meanings today are disconnected from what the words actually say, for example, *hang up the phone*, *roll down the car window*, and *you sound like a broken record*. Expressions can become obsolete, but God's truth will never be obsolete.

The Word of God is timeless. The Bible will be relevant "until heaven and earth pass away" and "until all things are accomplished." Not even the smallest part of a letter will be obsolete. Thus, Christians should study and teach what the whole Bible says.

> We proclaim [Christ], warning and teaching everyone with all wisdom, so that we may present everyone mature in Christ.
>
> Colossians 1:28 (CSB)

My mother taught Sunday School for many years. The women in her classes appreciated her dedication. Likewise, I am thankful for the men who taught me in Sunday School. I gained their love for the Word of God, a seed that has grown throughout my adult years. I think Sunday School teachers are the great ones in the Kingdom. Even though they are not famous, they are well-known to God.

Teaching in the Kingdom is best done by a life serving God. Examples from life are more powerful than abstract philosophy. The first step to becoming a teacher is to guard my own life by obeying the Word of God. The next step is to encourage others to do the same.

The Pharisees taught everyone to obey the Old Testament laws very carefully, but Jesus said their legalism was not good enough to get into the Kingdom of Heaven. What more did Jesus expect?

> The commandments, 'do not commit adultery;' 'do not murder;' 'do not steal;' 'do not covet;' and any other commandment, are summed up by this commandment: 'Love your neighbor as yourself.' Love does no wrong to a neighbor. Love, therefore, is the fulfillment of the law.
>
> Romans 13:9–10 (CSB)

In the 1960s, Joseph Fletcher's book, *Situation Ethics*,[3] stirred considerable controversy. It advocated setting aside the moral absolutes of the Bible in favor of "love." Popular culture embraced this as justification to do whatever they wanted. My peers seemed to be looking for ways to excuse open sexual immorality. *Situation Ethics* provided a philosophical basis for continuing to claim to be a Christian while disobeying the clear teaching of the Bible.

Some people resist obeying the Word of God, calling any restraint *legalism*. Rebellion is not a ticket for entering the Kingdom of Heaven, even if it is called *situation ethics*.

---

[3]Joseph Fletcher, *Situation Ethics: The New Morality* (Louisville, Kentucky: Westminster Press, 1966).

31

In the centuries after the Babylonian captivity, the rabbis' interpretation of the Law became legalistic and external, especially among the sect of the Pharisees in Jesus' time. Jesus said the legalism of the Pharisees is not a ticket for entering the Kingdom of Heaven.

Western Civilization has been shaped by ancient Greek (pagan) philosophies which analyzed life with logical reasoning. Such reasoning has a strictly human perspective. This also leads to legalism, making human logical reasoning more authoritative than what God says. Greek legalism is not a ticket for entering the Kingdom of Heaven either.

Many Christian commentators throughout the centuries have applied the Greek approach to the Scriptures, resulting in Christian legalism. Denominations have grown up, defending the legalism of their traditions. Modern commentators often invent new legalisms, while they claim to reject legalism. Christian legalism is not a ticket for entering the Kingdom of Heaven either.

Obedience comes from the heart, not from following legalistic rules. Jesus illustrated this principle with several examples of familiar rules. The first example is the law against murder.

Murder

Suppose a guy gets angry at work, but because he doesn't want to go to jail, he doesn't murder his coworker. Instead, when he gets home, he strikes the loyal loving family dog. This is called the *kick-the-dog syndrome*. Any innocent family member could be the next victim of the rage that began somewhere else.

Matthew 5:21–26 (CSB)[4]

---

21 You have heard that it was said to our ancestors, 'Do not murder,' and whoever murders will be subject to judgment. 22 But I tell you, everyone who is angry with his brother or sister will be subject to judgment. Whoever insults his brother or sister, will be subject to the court. Whoever says, 'You fool!' will be subject to hellfire. 23 So if you are offering your gift on the altar, and there you remember that your brother or sister has something against you, 24 leave your gift there in front of the altar. First go and be reconciled with your brother or sister, and then come and offer your gift. 25 Reach a settlement quickly with your adversary while you're on the way with him to the court, or your adversary will hand you over to the judge, and the judge to the officer, and you will be thrown into prison. 26 Truly I tell you, you will never get out of there until you have paid the last penny.

---

[4]Luke 12:58–59 is a parallel passage.

Jesus quoted one of the Ten Commandments,[5] but expanded its application to attitudes underlying any dispute. The whole Bible has much to say about anger.[6]

> Everyone who hates his brother or sister is a murderer, and you know that no murderer has eternal life residing in him.
>
> 1 John 3:15 (CSB)

Sin occurs first in the heart and later is expressed in action. Legalism only looks at the action. Anger comes from a hateful heart which is morally equivalent to murder, even though the victim, the object of the anger, does not die.

> 'Be angry and do not sin.' Don't let the sun go down on your anger.
>
> Ephesians 4:26 (CSB)

As a newly-wed, the first time my wife was angry with me, I immediately sat down close to her and tried to resolve the situation. She told me to give her space and time to cool off, so she wouldn't sin.

The word *anger* also refers to a natural human emotion. The issue is not my emotions, but how I respond to my emotions. As the Holy Spirit molds my character, anger gets displaced by compassion, so I am able to forgive any hurt immediately, and thus, avoid sinning.

> Let all bitterness, anger and wrath, shouting and slander be removed from you, along with all malice. And be kind and compassionate to one another, forgiving one another, just as God also forgave you in Christ.
>
> Ephesians 4:31–32 (CSB)

Under United States law, *defamation* is intentional false communication that harms a victim's reputation or induces hostile opinions or feelings against the victim. *Libel* is defamation that can be seen, such as writing, and *slander* is defamation that is spoken and heard. American courts consider these civil wrongs, not crimes, so lawsuits are the legal mechanism for redress. Jesus was addressing any kind of ill communication, not just legal wrongs, and he referred to judgment in the court of heaven, not just the Jewish courts of his day.

Apparently, in Jesus' time, if slander was phrased a certain way, "Raca!" (perhaps meaning empty head),[7] then you were liable in court, but if you phrased your slander differently, "You fool!" you were not liable. This was just legal gymnastics. The way you phrase slander doesn't matter to God. It is still slander. Slander flow from an angry heart. It is not just a civil legal offense.

When I substitute kindness, compassion, and forgiveness for bitterness, anger, and slander, I am living in the Kingdom, but disputes will still happen. How should I react?

---

[5] Exodus 20:13.
[6] For example, Ephesians 4:26–27 and Colossians 3:8.
[7] 5:22 (CSB) footnote.

> As it is, to have legal disputes against one another is already a defeat for you. Why not rather be wronged? Why not rather be cheated?
>
> 1 Corinthians 6:7 (CSB)

Americans are very aware of their rights. Many people wrap their self-esteem with their rights. Any small infraction gets a big reaction as though it's a major assault on one's identity. A casual word can easily be construed as slander and even lead to lawsuits.

When I feel I have been treated unfairly, my natural response is to become angry and to assert my rights. I might slander my opponent, and then he is probably offended. My slander against my brother will not only interfere with my relationship with my brother, but also will block my relationship with God, represented by a "gift at the altar" in 5:23–24. Slander has terrible consequences for me.

If I have slandered someone in my anger, he may sue me and take me to court. Jesus recommended settling out of court, because the penalty of the court will be much more severe. Confession, apology, and forgiveness will restore a brotherly relationship.

If I feel I've been treated unfairly, I don't need to get angry. I should be willing to give up my rights to benefit others. I will defend the rights of others, but I don't need to assert my rights to salve my pride. However, in some situations, asserting one's rights may be necessary to prevent future abuse.

The obvious way to prevent trouble is to control my anger and not slander anyone. I've been learning to avoid anger and to avoid hurting others when I feel angry. Living in the Kingdom means being sensitive to others' feelings and not letting anger become sin. I can afford to be generous.

Adultery

In the twenty-first century, sexual immorality is openly advocated throughout Western Civilization. Adultery is common. A majority have sex before marriage, often with a series of partners. Pornography is readily available. Movies and TV portray immorality as normal. Public figures in entertainment, sports, and politics are not expected to have chaste lives. The Kingdom of Heaven is different.

Matthew 5:27–30 (CSB)

---

27 You have heard that it was said, 'Do not commit adultery.' 28 But I tell you, everyone who looks at a woman lustfully has already committed adultery with her in his heart. 29 If your right eye causes you to sin, gouge it out and throw it away. For it is better that you lose one of the parts of your body than for your whole body to be thrown into hell. 30 And if your right hand causes you to sin, cut it

off and throw it away. For it is better that you lose one of the parts
of your body than for your whole body to go into hell.

Jesus applied Kingdom principles to adultery. He emphasized the importance of avoiding sexual sin by using hyperbole when he spoke of maiming
one's body.

Do not love the world or the things in the world. If anyone loves
the world, the love of the Father is not in him. For everything in
the world—the lust of the flesh, the lust of the eyes, and the pride
in one's possessions—is not from the Father, but is from the world.
1 John 2:15–16 (CSB)

"Do not commit adultery" is one of the Ten Commandments.[8] It clearly
refers to actions. Law in the Kingdom of Heaven concerns the heart. Sexual lust
in the heart may lead to adultery in action. This passage in Matthew applies to
all kinds of sexual immorality, not just the narrow sense of *adultery*.[9]

Controlling one's eyes in the area of sexuality is a major challenge for anyone past the age of puberty. Sexual enticement is everywhere and is used to
sell all kinds of things, even soap. Popular culture glamorizes sex and pres-
sures people toward a promiscuous lifestyle. It all begins with the eyes. Visual
temptation progresses to lustful imagination, lustful look, sexual immorality
in the heart, and eventually, sexual immorality in action.

But each person is tempted when he is drawn away and enticed by
his own evil desire. Then after desire has conceived, it gives birth
to sin, and when sin is fully grown, it gives birth to death.
James 1:14–15 (CSB)

I am not enticed to think about sin by the round ball in my head, my eye.
The flesh and bones of my hand do not automatically do some sin. Physical
things like an eye or hand do not affect whether the heart sins. Because the
origin of lust is in the soul, getting rid of the implement for sin in action, an
eye or hand, will not solve the sin issue in the heart. The desire to sin is in the
heart and it motivates actions.

Refusing to be entrapped by sexual immorality is more important than losing my eye or my hand. Even though I live in a sexually immoral culture, God
has promised such temptations will not overwhelm me. God will provide a
way of escape.[10] He helps me focus my attention on good things. He helps me
carefully select what I read. He gives me understanding that the proper place
for sex is in marriage.

---

[8]Exodus 20:14.
[9]Galatians 5:19, Colossians 3:5, and 1 Thessalonians 4:3–5.
[10]1 Corinthians 10:13.

Divorce

Hansel and Joan had a rocky marriage which ended in divorce. All involved had suffered. Later, they both became believers a thousand miles apart. After no contact for more than fifteen years, they reconciled and remarried. The wounds of their earlier marriage were healed.

Matthew 5:31–32 (CSB)[11]

---

31 It was also said, 'Whoever divorces his wife must give her a written notice of divorce.' 32 But I tell you, everyone who divorces his wife, except in a case of sexual immorality, causes her to commit adultery. And whoever marries a divorced woman commits adultery.

Some commentators' outlines combine this passage with the previous one on adultery, because they both relate to marriage and the introductory wording here does not follow exactly the pattern of the other topics. However, it is convenient to discuss them separately.

> What is the one seeking? Godly offspring. So watch yourselves carefully, so that no one acts treacherously against the wife of his youth.
> "If he hates and divorces his wife," says the Lord God of Israel, "he covers his garment with injustice," says the Lord of Armies. Therefore, watch yourselves carefully, and do not act treacherously.
> Malachi 2:15–16 (CSB)

In Malachi's time, the people were disappointed God was not answering their prayers. God replied through Malachi that men were divorcing their wives unjustly. Ungodliness in marriage and then divorce hinders couples from raising godly children, so God hates divorce.

Jesus compared divorce and adultery. Breaking faith is the sin common to both. In Jesus' day, the husband could divorce his wife for almost any reason. A man could break faith through divorce, but a woman couldn't. She could break faith through sexual immorality though.

Jesus pointed to the custom, authorized in the Torah, of giving a divorced woman a certificate saying she was indeed single even though she was no longer a virgin. Usually she was the victim, so the certificate showed she was legally independent from her former husband. But this legal rule did not solve the problems caused by divorce. Jesus used the certificate as a rhetorical stepping stone to emphasize the damage divorce causes. One sin just leads to another.

Divorce damages all who are involved, beginning with the husband and wife and spreading to children, extended family, and friends. That's a reason

---

[11]Mark 10:1–12 and Luke 16:18 are similar but in different settings.

God hates divorce. Divorce has no place in Kingdom living. The grace of God is sufficient to solve all relationship problems a married couple may have, but they both must submit to that grace for it to be effective.

Like other areas where sin destroys, the grace of God can heal and restore those damaged by divorce. The hallmark of Kingdom living is restoration and renewal.

Oaths

I went to a seminar that recommended setting goals for your life. "Where do you want to be in one year, five years, and ten years?" I was reluctant to be specific, because Jesus warned about making oaths.

Matthew 5:33–37 (CSB)[12]

---

33 Again, you have heard that it was said to our ancestors, 'You must not break your oath, but you must keep your oaths to the Lord.' 34 But I tell you, don't take an oath at all: either by heaven, because it is God's throne; 35 or by the earth, because it is his footstool; or by Jerusalem, because it is the city of the great King. 36 Do not swear by your head, because you cannot make a single hair white or black. 37 But let your 'yes' mean 'yes,' and your 'no' mean 'no.' Anything more than this is from the evil one.

Jesus referred to the Torah.[13] Oaths were allowed, but it was important to fulfill oaths to the Lord. Some oaths in the Old Testament were intended to emphasize the speaker's determination to do something. Other oaths asserted the speaker's truthfulness, when no one but God could be sure.

For example, King Saul made a foolish oath before his battle with the Philistines.[14] He commanded his troops not to eat until the battle was over, and vowed to kill any soldier who did. His son Jonathan did not hear the oath, so he ate some honey in the forest. At the end of the day, Saul almost killed Jonathan to fulfill the oath, but the people rescued Jonathan. The oath was Saul's attempt to show he was determined to vanquish the Philistines.

If I do make plans for the future, I won't confidently say, "I will do such and such." I must always qualify my plans with "If the Lord wills."

Come now, you who say, "Today or tomorrow we will travel to such and such a city and spend a year there and do business and make a profit." Yet you do not know what tomorrow will bring—what your life will be! For you are like vapor that appears for a little while, then vanishes.

---

[12]See also James 5:12 and Ecclesiastes 5:2–7.
[13]Deuteronomy 23:21–23.
[14]1 Samuel 14:23–46.

Instead, you should say, "If the Lord wills, we will live and do this or that." But as it is, you boast in your arrogance. All such boasting is evil.

James 4:13–16 (CSB)

Making an oath about future actions is foolish and disrespectful of the sovereignty of God. We humans can never guarantee anything will happen in the future. The root issue regarding an oath is the arrogance of thinking I am like God. I don't have any reservations about taking an oath in a courtroom which ends with *so help me God*. This phrase acknowledges our human frailty. Human thinking and perception are error prone and the future is uncertain. The simple alternative to oaths is just telling the truth.

But speaking the truth in love, let us grow in every way into him who is the head—Christ.

Ephesians 4:15 (CSB)

While reviewing a draft, I discovered a student in our university research group had copied some of my writing as if it were her own. It would have been easy to ignore this issue, but I told her the truth, plagiarism is unethical. She was disappointed the writing needed correction, but I helped her fix it.

By letting my word *yes* always mean yes, and my *no* always mean no, I am free to just tell the truth without worrying about convincing listeners I am being truthful. I must always speak truthfully, but without making arrogant oaths. I will speak truthfully about my past experiences. I will speak truthfully about my present thoughts and feelings. I will speak truthfully about my intentions and hopes for the future.

Even though I am committed to always speak truthfully, there are many situations where remaining silent is better for all concerned. Even when asked a question, I don't have to answer. Living truthfully does not give anyone else the right to know all the time what I think and know. Kingdom living is a truthful lifestyle, without deception, without any need for oaths.

Revenge

One of my neighbors told me another neighbor had cheated him in a car repair deal. His revenge was a big hand-painted sign on the disabled car, "So-and-so is a thief!" The sign was on display for over two years. The vengeful neighbor later apologized for the display.

Matthew 5:38–42 (CSB)

38 You have heard that it was said, 'An eye for an eye and a tooth for a tooth.' 39 But I tell you, don't resist an evildoer. On the contrary, if anyone slaps you on your right cheek, turn the other to him also. 40 As for the one who wants to sue you and take away your shirt,

let him have your coat as well. 41 And if anyone forces you to go one mile, go with him two. 42 Give to the one who asks you, and don't turn away from the one who wants to borrow from you.

"An eye for an eye and a tooth for a tooth," is a quote from the Torah[15] which explains the standard of justice to be used by courts in ancient Israel. The phrase *resist an evildoer* in verse 39 probably refers to a court of law as well.[16]

> Friends, do not avenge yourselves; instead, leave room for God's wrath, because it is written, "Vengeance belongs to me; I will repay," says the Lord.
>
> Romans 12:19 (CSB)

The principle of "an eye for an eye" is often used to justify revenge. Someone might say, "I have been offended, therefore I have a right to take revenge." He thinks the payback should be as hurtful as the original offense or even more so. "An eye for an eye" was only a legal rule for ancient Israel. This means it does not apply to personal offenses. Revenge is sin, because it usurps God's prerogative to administer justice.

After quoting the Torah, Jesus proceeded to give examples from everyday life rather than courtroom situations, namely, an insult, a lawsuit, oppression (by the Roman army), and someone who asks for a loan. In each situation, one is tempted to take revenge against one's opponent. In each case, the Kingdom reaction is generosity rather than revenge.

Insults. A friend told her husband not to pop her anymore with his belt when he was changing clothes. He did so anyway out of spite. The next thing he knew, a judo move had put him on the floor. An inconsiderate attitude results in insult and revenge.

> Finally, all of you be like-minded and sympathetic, love one another, and be compassionate and humble, not paying back evil for evil or insult for insult but, on the contrary, giving a blessing, since you were called for this, so that you may inherit a blessing.
>
> 1 Peter 3:8–9 (CSB)

The phrase *strike you on the right cheek* means a slap,[17] which is an insult, rather than an act of violence. The natural reaction to an insult is to strike back with another insult. Kids throw dirty names at each other. Adults give backhanded compliments.

---

[15] Exodus 21:24, Leviticus 24:20, and Deuteronomy 19:21.

[16] Carson, p. 155. Elsewhere in the gospels, Jesus approves of getting justice in court.

[17] Carson, p. 156.

Revenge over insults is not Kingdom living. As a humble citizen of the Kingdom, I can afford to be insulted, even doubly insulted, right and left, without making an issue of the incident. Peter said the reaction to an insult should be to bless the other person. As a citizen of the Kingdom, I can afford to be generous.

Lawsuits. Two families in my neighborhood were enemies due to offenses and revenge. They used the homeowners' association meetings as a battleground. Each side tried to get neighbors to vote for their side. Their dispute eventually escalated to threatening a lawsuit and a countersuit. My neighbors were not believers, but sometimes Christians get entangled in such disputes.

> If any of you has a dispute against another, how dare you take it to court before the unrighteous, and not before the saints?
> 1 Corinthians 6:1 (CSB)

The Christians in Corinth were fighting with each other in secular courts. Paul reprimanded them for their legal actions. Irrespective of whether an evildoer or a believer brings the lawsuit, the Kingdom response is the same. Respond to injustice with generosity instead of revenge. As a citizen of the Kingdom, I can afford to be generous.

Oppression. An international student went to get a driver's license at the Division of Motor Vehicles (DMV). The clerk required a letter certifying he was a student. However, no one in the university was authorized to write such a letter. Then he went to the DMV office in the next town and found they did not require a letter. The multitude of little hassles by government agencies add up to oppression of the defenseless.

> Again, I observed all the acts of oppression being done under the sun. Look at the tears of those who are oppressed; they have no one to comfort them. Power is with those who oppress them; they have no one to comfort them.
> Ecclesiastes 4:1 (CSB)

The phrase *forces you to go one mile* probably refers to oppression by the Roman army.[18] The natural reaction of a first century Jew would be outrage against the Romans. Rather than react with bitterness, Jesus said to give more than was required. Jesus' example may have been specific to his day, but his teaching is applicable to all kinds of oppression.

Government at all levels has an endless assortment of regulations, zoning rules, building codes, ordinances, and legislation. It's easy to run afoul of somebody's rules. When a government agency forces the helpless to conform, there is usually no recourse. The oppressed may long for revenge, but must just suffer through.

---

[18]Carson, p. 156.

When I feel oppressed, the Kingdom response is to give willingly more than was required. As a citizen of the Kingdom, I can afford to be generous.

Loans. A guy came to my door asking for ten dollars for gas. He said his car was over on the next block. So, I got out my lawn mower's gas can. Then he started making excuses about how my gas can wouldn't fit his car, which I knew was not true. I guess he didn't really want gas.

This guy was trying to deceive me. When I give out of love, the evil person's antics are powerless. I don't have to comply with the demands of every manipulative person in my life. As a citizen of the Kingdom, I am free to say "Yes," or "No."

On another occasion, a car stopped in front of my house. When I went to investigate, the elderly man getting out said, "I ran out of gas." So, I got my lawn mower's gas can, and emptied it into his gas tank. He thanked me and drove on his way.

This man didn't have time to ask for gas, because I was already prepared to give him some. I can afford to be kind to someone in need. I can afford to loan something without expecting it to be returned. As a citizen of the Kingdom, I can afford to be generous.

Enemies

Dietrich Bonhoeffer had enemies in Nazi Germany. He faced a hostile interrogator in prison, and Hitler personally ordered his execution. Bonhoeffer said, "In the New Testament our enemies are those who harbor hostility against us, not those against whom we cherish hostility."[19]

Matthew 5:43–48 (CSB)

---

43 You have heard that it was said, 'Love your neighbor' and hate your enemy. 44 But I tell you, love your enemies and pray for those who persecute you, 45 so that you may be children of your Father in heaven. For he causes his sun to rise on the evil and the good, and sends rain on the righteous and the unrighteous. 46 For if you love those who love you, what reward will you have? Don't even the tax collectors do the same? 47 And if you greet only your brothers and sisters, what are you doing out of the ordinary? Don't even the Gentiles do the same? 48 Be perfect, therefore, as your heavenly Father is perfect.

The proverb Jesus quoted is not in the Old Testament, but it is the way most people feel. *Love your neighbor* is in the Torah, but *hate your enemy* is not. What does God think about his enemies?

---

[19] Bonhoeffer, p. 164.

> But God proves his own love for us in that while we were still sin-
> ners, Christ died for us.
>
> Romans 5:8 (CSB)

In a small Bible study group, the leader asked each person to share his
religious background. Angie said, "Heathen." Growing up, Angie didn't have
any Christian influence, except her grandmother's short visit once each year.
But God still loved her. She became a believer as an adult, and her family
became Christians, too.

Because God loves his enemies, he is kind to them. The sun rising and rain
falling are gifts to all, including God's enemies. The heavenly Father expects
his children to exhibit his character. I was God's enemy in my sin, but Jesus
died for me. Therefore, as a citizen of the Kingdom, I must love my enemies,
too. I must be like my heavenly Father, even though enemies are real.

> [Jesus said:] If the world hates you, understand that it hated me
> before it hated you. If you were of the world, the world would love
> you as its own. However, because you are not of the world, but I
> have chosen you out of it, the world hates you.
>
> John 15:18–19 (CSB)

If I love my enemies, then it is impossible to say who is an enemy by how
I feel. If I instantly forgive, and pray for a hostile person, then I don't think of
that person as an enemy. I remind myself that sinners are victims of their own
sin and that God loves them anyway.

> First of all, then, I urge that petitions, prayers, intercessions, and
> thanksgivings be made for everyone, for kings and all those who
> are in authority, so that we may lead a tranquil and quiet life in all
> godliness and dignity.
>
> 1 Timothy 2:1–2 (CSB)

Government officials sometimes act like anonymous enemies. In New Testament times, they were pagans who sometimes persecuted Christians. Paul
told Timothy to pray for all kinds of government officials.

> Christian love draws no distinction between one enemy and an-
> other, except that the more bitter our enemy's hatred, the greater
> his need of love...
>   [By praying,] we are doing vicariously for them what they can-
> not do for themselves.
>
> Dietrich Bonhoeffer[20]

As a citizen of the Kingdom, I must pray for the welfare of my enemies,
praying for blessings, not curses, and not judgment. When I pray for my enemies, I am interceding for them in a way they can't for themselves.
    Jesus said I should give love to more than just my friends and family.

---

[20]Bonhoeffer, pp. 164,166.

> My brothers and sisters, do not show favoritism as you hold on to
> the faith in our glorious Lord Jesus Christ.
>
> James 2:1 (CSB)

I enjoy connecting with friends on Facebook. Some of my friends use Facebook as a platform to air their political views. I often wonder if they would still be my friends if they knew my political views.

In the world, people love their friends and family. In some cultures, *friend* is defined by tribe, race, or class. In modern culture, *friend* and *enemy* are often defined by political ideology, religion or anti-religion, social background, lifestyle, and so on.

Hostility between groups is often expressed in jokes that denigrate the other group. This is especially obvious with racial or ethnic jokes. Political jokes are often vicious also.

In the Kingdom, none of these categories count. God is not a respecter of persons. He is perfect in love. He completely loves. As a citizen of the Kingdom, I must do so also.

Law in the Kingdom

The Pharisees tried to obey the Old Testament laws precisely, but their legalism could not fulfill its purpose. Jesus came to be that fulfillment. He is the source of our faith.[21] His life demonstrates the truth of God's Word. It will never be obsolete. The Pharisees' legalism could not earn entrance to the Kingdom of Heaven. Greek legalism could not either. Christian legalism can't either. Obedience must come from the heart to fulfill the Law's purpose. Jesus illustrated this with several familiar laws.

Murder. Anger in the heart is the root of murder in action. The Bible teaches me to avoid anger, and if I feel angry, to avoid hurting others. If I am sensitive to others' feelings, angry reactions will dissipate and will not become sin.

Adultery. Lustful eyes are the root of all kinds of sexual immorality. Even though I live in a sexually immoral culture, God helps me focus my attention on good things, and his Word shows me the proper place of sex in marriage.

Divorce. God hates divorce, because it damages all who are involved. But where sin destroys, the grace of God can heal and restore those damaged by divorce.

Oaths. Jesus said to avoid making oaths. It is presumptuous to be so certain about the future or about human perception and memory. When I live a truthful lifestyle, without deception, I don't need oaths.

---

[21]Hebrews 12:2.

Revenge. Revenge is the natural reaction to a wound. Jesus taught me to be generous when someone insults me, sues me in court, oppresses me, or asks to borrow from me. As a citizen of the Kingdom, I can afford to be generous.

Enemies. God loves his enemies. As a child of God, I will imitate my heavenly Father. An enemy is someone who is hostile toward me, not someone against whom I'm hostile. It is easier to pray for an enemy when I recognize sinners are victims of their own sin.

Law in the Kingdom. The Pharisees taught strict external obedience to rules, but Jesus taught obedience from a faithful heart. Because the Old Testament is fulfilled by Jesus, legalism is not necessary.

4

Religion in the Kingdom

Our activity must be visible, but never done for the sake of making it visible...

From whom are we to hide the visibility of our discipleship? Certainly not from other men, for we are told to let them see our light. No. We are to hide it from ourselves. Our task is simply to keep on following.

Dietrich Bonhoeffer[1]

Jesus taught the disciples, "Let your light shine before others,"[2] and "Be careful not to practice your righteousness in front of others."[3] These seem to be a contradiction. From whom are we to hide our good works? Bonhoeffer said we are to hide them from ourselves. What is my motivation? Do I want God to get the glory? Or do I seek the credit? If my motive is just to follow Jesus, then I won't think my good works are significant.

The disciples were accustomed to doing various commendable religious acts. This chapter discusses what Jesus thought about such actions. His examples were giving to the poor, praying, and fasting.[4]

Righteousness in public

As I walked through a park, I came upon a stone bench that had carved on it, "Daphne (Daphy Jean) Bray (1918–1993) When most people looked for rainbows you took pleasure in the rain." Apparently, she was beloved and respected in the community, so someone put the bench there to preserve her memory.

---

[1] Bonhoeffer, pp. 175, 176.
[2] 5:16 (CSB).
[3] 6:1 (CSB).
[4] The outline groups the examples in 6:1–18, because they all begin with "When you do ..."

Matthew 6:1 (CSB)

---

1 Be careful not to practice your righteousness in front of others to be seen by them. Otherwise, you have no reward with your Father in heaven.

This verse as an introduction to the topic of religious acts in the Kingdom.[5]

> But know this: Hard times will come in the last days. For people will be lovers of self, … holding to the form of godliness but denying its power. Avoid these people.
>
> 2 Timothy 3:1–5 (CSB)

There are many kinds of good works respectable church people do which benefit the community, such as picking up trash on the roadside, erecting new playground equipment at a park, serving Thanksgiving dinners to the homeless, and donating toys for poor children at Christmas. Some might think such activities win a reward from God. They don't realize hoping to win recognition from the community means God ignores them.

Fame is a fleeting reward. People promptly forget whatever good thing you did. A sports fan might say, "You may have been champion last year, but what have you won lately?" In ancient times, kings would build great monuments, so people would not forget their accomplishments, only to have the monuments crumble over time and be buried by the encroaching desert.

Jesus covered three examples of religious actions (righteousness) that were normal practices for his disciples. In each case, trying to win the praise of men corrupts a good action. A pure motive is a necessary ingredient for a religious act to count as a good work in God's eyes. Kingdom living does not seek fame or congratulations from people, even if it is well-deserved by worldly standards.

When you give to the poor

If you give enough money, a university will name a college after you. If you can't afford that much, how about a plaque on a chair in a lecture hall? Still too expensive? How about a brick in the sidewalk with your name on it? Charitable giving in the world will get you fame, honor, and maybe even a bronze plaque. The accolades may stroke your ego, but will not gain the favor of God.

---

[5]Carson (p. 163) explained that some manuscripts of Matthew have the Greek word for *alms* in 6:1 and 6:2. The Greek word *eleemosynen* (*Strong's* No. 1654) means giving to the poor. The KJV and others are based on these manuscripts. Other manuscripts have the Greek word for *righteousness* in 6:1 but the word for *alms* in 6:2. The Greek word *dikaiosynen* (*Strong's* No. 1343) means acts of righteousness. The CSB, NIV, and other modern translations prefer these manuscripts.

Matthew 6:2–4 (CSB)

---

2 So whenever you give to the poor, don't sound a trumpet before you, as the hypocrites do in the synagogues and on the streets, to be applauded by people. Truly I tell you, they have their reward. 3 But when you give to the poor, don't let your left hand know what your right hand is doing, 4 so that your giving may be in secret. And your Father who sees in secret will reward you.

Jesus assumed his disciples will give to the poor. This passage is about having a proper attitude when giving.[6]

> Kindness to the poor is a loan to the Lord,
> and he will give a reward to the lender.
>
> Proverbs 19:17 (CSB)

Sometimes, sadly, giving in the church is done in the worldly way with certificates and plaques to commemorate the giver. There is no lasting reward for such. God is not impressed by how worthy the charitable cause was, nor by how much was given.[7] God looks at the heart of the giver.

Jesus recommended giving anonymously to the poor, so only God would know what was done. In modern society, I can trust the bookkeeper at church not to disclose my gift to the public, and the US Internal Revenue Service is not going to trumpet my tax-deductible charitable giving either. I will give in such a way that I won't receive any praise that will boost my pride.

God sees giving to the poor. He sees the humble heart behind the giving, and he rewards in his own way. Kingdom living means giving to the needy without public recognition.

When you pray

The Martin Luther King Day Breakfast was about to begin. A local pastor had been recruited to pray aloud something that would offend no one. At the end of the festivities, another local pastor prayed a benediction. Many civic events have professional invocation and benediction prayers. Does God listen to such prayers?

Matthew 6:5–15 (CSB)[8]

---

5 Whenever you pray, you must not be like the hypocrites, because they love to pray standing in the synagogues and on the street corners to be seen by people. Truly I tell you, they have their reward.

---

[6]Bible scholars are unsure what custom the phrase *sound a trumpet* refers to (Carson, pp. 163–164).

[7]Mark 12:41–44.

[8]Luke 11:2–4 is a parallel passage.

6 But when you pray, go into your private room, shut your door, and pray to your Father who is in secret. And your Father who sees in secret will reward you. 7 When you pray, don't babble like the Gentiles, since they imagine they'll be heard for their many words. 8 Don't be like them, because your Father knows the things you need before you ask him.

9 Therefore, you should pray like this:

> Our Father in heaven,
> your name be honored as holy.
> 10 Your kingdom come.
> Your will be done
> 11 on earth as it is in heaven.
> Give us today our daily bread.
> 12 And forgive us our debts,
> as we also have forgiven our debtors.
> 13 And do not bring us into temptation,
> but deliver us from the evil one.
> [For yours is the kingdom and the power and the glory forever.
> Amen.][9]

14 For if you forgive others their offenses, your heavenly Father will forgive you as well. 15 But if you don't forgive others, your Father will not forgive your offenses.

Verses 9 through 13 are called the *Lord's Prayer* or the *Our Father*. Jesus assumed his disciples will pray, so he gave guidance on where to pray, how to pray, and what to pray.

Where to pray. Jesus recommended praying in private. God hears private prayers.

> Lord, you have heard the desire of the humble;
> you will strengthen their hearts.
> You will listen carefully.

> Psalm 10:17 (CSB)

When I was a teenager, everyone assumed the pastor would do all the praying aloud at church. The pastor was a professional. He had been to seminary. His prayers were much more eloquent than anybody else's. People thought maybe God answers professional eloquent prayers better.

Today, lay people like me often pray in public. People will probably think I'm pious if I recite eloquent prayers. Jesus said praying in public to be seen

---

[9]The doxology is missing from the oldest manuscripts, but has been embraced by worshipers for centuries (Carson, p. 174).

is not what counts. God is not interested in eloquence. God is looking for an honest humble heart. Public acclaim, "That was a good prayer!" detracts from honest prayer.

Daniel prayed openly, but not for show.[10] When I'm asked to pray aloud in a group setting, I just try to pray the same way I pray in private, ignoring what others may think.

How to pray. Jesus recommended simple short prayers. He said the pagan's style of wordy praying won't get an answer.

> So [the priests of Baal] took the bull that [Elijah] gave them, prepared it, and called on the name of Baal from morning until noon, saying, "Baal, answer us!" But there was no sound; no one answered. Then they danced around the altar they had made.
>
> At noon Elijah mocked them. He said, "Shout loudly, for he's a god! Maybe he's thinking it over; maybe he has wandered away; or maybe he's on the road. Perhaps he's sleeping and will wake up!" They shouted loudly, and cut themselves with knives and spears, according to their custom, until blood gushed over them. All afternoon they kept on raving until the offering of the evening sacrifice, but there was no sound; no one answered, no one paid attention.
>
> 1 Kings 18:26–29 (CSB)

I received an email from a friend asking for prayer about a heart-touching need she had read about in the news. Her email went out to almost everyone she knew to recruit a great army of prayer warriors. Maybe if there is one person in all that army who is more righteous than most, God will answer. Maybe if we add everyone's prayers together, the quantity of prayers will move God to answer. Maybe "more is better."

Christians have prayed together in groups since the beginning. Groups praying together is good. Friends interceding for friends is good. Christians joining in prayer for the community is good. The benefit of praying in a group is God touches the hearts of the prayer warriors, not because more prayer makes God respond.

Jesus said the pagans babble their prayers, thinking many words will make them more effective. Many words are not necessary, because God already knows what we need. "More is better" is a pagan idea of prayer.

When I was a teenager, I learned to pray aloud with "sentence prayers" which were short and conveyed just one idea. Each person in a group would speak up with just one sentence as one thought came to mind. The sentences were not eloquent. When I read the Lord's Prayer, it sounds like sentence prayer is the style Jesus had in mind.

---

[10]Daniel 6:10.

What to pray. The Lord's Prayer is a model for us.[11] It demonstrates what to pray by suggesting some topics. Of course, my heavenly Father wants to hear about any topic I may be concerned about.

> [Jesus said:] I tell you, everything you pray and ask for—believe that you have received it and it will be yours.
>
> Mark 11:24 (CSB)

I am confident my prayers will be answered, because I am an adopted child of God. He is my heavenly Father. I will praise him forever for his holiness, his sovereignty, and his justice. My concerns from day to day are like the petitions of the model prayer. I am dependent on the Lord for sustenance, forgiveness, and deliverance. The doxology at the end summarizes his majesty.

> [Jesus said:] And whenever you stand praying, if you have anything against anyone, forgive him, so that your Father in heaven will also forgive you your wrongdoing.
>
> Mark 11:25 (CSB)

While I was sitting in my easy chair, reading the Bible and praying over the usual things, I realized I was still upset Toyota USA had refused to pay for my transmission repair, even though it was their fault. I knew I had to forgive them.

One of the sentence prayers of the Lord's Prayer asks for forgiveness. After the prayer, Jesus emphasized how important it is for me to forgive others. An honest heart cleansed by the forgiveness of God is the prerequisite to effective prayer.

I want my prayers to be effective, so whenever I feel offended or wounded by someone else, I must immediately get past my feelings and forgive. An occasion to pray may come up at any time. Kingdom living means praying simply and keeping my heart clean and ready.

When you fast

I invited my friend to join a group for lunch after church. He was hesitant, but I insisted. At the food court in the mall, he only had a drink. Then I realized he was fasting, but he didn't want anyone to notice.

Matthew 6:16–18 (CSB)

---

16 Whenever you fast, don't be gloomy like the hypocrites. For they make their faces unattractive so that their fasting is obvious to people. Truly I tell you, they have their reward. 17 But when you fast, put oil on your head and wash your face, 18 so that your fasting

---

[11]There are many excellent books expounding on the Lord's Prayer in detail, so there is no need to do that here.

isn't obvious to others but to your Father who is in secret. And your Father who sees in secret will reward you.

Jesus assumed everyone knows fasting is a worthwhile spiritual activity, when done properly.[12]

> I cannot tolerate anyone
> with haughty eyes or an arrogant heart.
>
> Psalm 101:5 (CSB)

If I let everyone know I'm fasting, then I'm really trying to impress them with how pious I think I am. There is no reward from the heavenly Father. The only reward is congratulations from people. Jesus criticized the hypocrites who pretended to be in great discomfort. When fasting is done privately, without a public show, God knows the action and sees the humble heart.[13]

Fasting is an uncomfortable activity. This teaching of Jesus applies to any uncomfortable activity we do for spiritual reasons. There are many activities that are spiritually good but are inconvenient or uncomfortable, for example, giving up my seat on the bus and standing the rest of my ride, or giving someone a ride home, miles out of my way. If I let everyone know how I'm "suffering for God" then their sympathy is my only reward. If I don't let anyone know about my discomfort, but just bear it, God will reward me.

Most of the time, I don't need to go to great lengths to hide my activities. God is not interested in who knows about my fasting or my good works. He cares about my heart. Am I looking for sympathy? Am I manipulating others to think highly of me? Am I spiritually arrogant? Kingdom living means having a simple attitude, doing what's right, never expecting other people to notice, and just going on with life.

Religion in the Kingdom

What is the place of religious acts in the Kingdom of Heaven? Religious people emphasize doing things to please God. What does God really care about?

> [Jesus] also told this parable to some who trusted in themselves that they were righteous and looked down on everyone else: "Two men went up to the temple to pray, one a Pharisee and the other a tax collector. The Pharisee was standing and praying like this about himself: 'God, I thank you that I'm not like other people—greedy, unrighteous, adulterers, or even like this tax collector. I fast twice a week; I give a tenth of everything I get.'

---

[12] An exposition of doctrine about fasting is outside the scope of this book.

[13] In first century Judea, washing one's face and putting oil in one's hair were normal good grooming.

"But the tax collector, standing far off, would not even raise his eyes to heaven but kept striking his chest and saying, 'God, have mercy on me, a sinner!' I tell you, this one went down to his house justified rather than the other; because everyone who exalts himself will be humbled, but the one who humbles himself will be exalted."

Luke 18:9–14 (CSB)

The Pharisee in this parable was a respected member of the community. Tax collectors were despised. The Pharisee fasted and he tithed which are certainly worthwhile religious activities. He obeyed all the rules Pharisees thought were important. But he did not receive forgiveness like the tax collector did. God rewarded the tax collector's repentance. God wants religious activities to be done with humble hearts. Jesus illustrated this point with three examples: giving to the poor, praying, and fasting.

Giving to the poor. Jesus recommended giving to the needy anonymously. God sees what is done and rewards in his own way, even though there is no bronze plaque.

Praying. Jesus recommended praying in private. Honest prayer is more important than public acclaim. Eloquent prayers don't impress God. An army of prayer warriors doesn't impress God. "More is better" is a pagan idea of prayer. The Lord's Prayer is my model, short and simple from a heart cleansed by forgiveness. If I do pray aloud in a group setting, I will pray like I do in private.

Fasting. God sees me when fasting privately. Jesus' teaching on fasting is applicable to any uncomfortable or inconvenient activity done for spiritual reasons. God's approval is more important than looking like I'm pious.

Religion in the Kingdom. Giving to the poor, praying, and fasting were normal practices for Jesus' disciples and should be for me, too. Jesus said to do such good things privately, because trying to impress others will corrupt good actions. I'm not interested in becoming a famous Christian. Kingdom living means doing good things without expecting people to notice.

5

Priorities in the Kingdom

The way to misuse our possessions is to use them as an insurance against the morrow... The only way to win assurance is by leaving tomorrow entirely in the hands of God and by receiving from him all we need for today.

Dietrich Bonhoeffer[1]

When I finish a home project, some screws and clips are usually left over. I keep them for years and years. "I might need that someday!" If the world falls apart, I'm sure I'll have the right size screw. The way I use possessions shows whether my priority is trusting God or trying to assure the future by my own efforts.

This chapter discusses four passages that all say, "Do not do such and such." They reveal priorities in the Kingdom of Heaven that are the opposite of patterns in the world.[2]

Do not serve money

I tend to collect books and magazines. They are my treasures. Each time I moved, I had to box them up and haul them to the next place. The old magazines were starting to turn yellow. I had too many. The last time I moved, I gave away almost all my professional books and magazines. It was hard to let go of my treasures. Jesus recommended not collecting treasures here on earth.

Matthew 6:19–24 (CSB)[3]

---

19 Don't store up for yourselves treasures on earth, where moth and rust destroy and where thieves break in and steal. 20 But store up

---

[1]Bonhoeffer, pp. 197–198.
[2]The outline groups the passages in 6:19–7:6 together, because they have similar wording.
[3]Luke 12:34 and Luke 11:34–36 are parallel passages.

for yourselves treasures in heaven, where neither moth nor rust destroys, and where thieves don't break in and steal. 21 For where your treasure is, there your heart will be also.

22 The eye is the lamp of the body. If your eye is healthy, your whole body will be full of light. 23 But if your eye is bad, your whole body will be full of darkness. So if the light within you is darkness, how deep is that darkness!

24 No one can serve two masters, since either he will hate one and love the other, or he will be devoted to one and despise the other. You cannot serve both God and money.

Treasure. Jesus gave three illustrations of treasure in this life: clothes, metal tools, and household valuables.

> A greedy one is in a hurry for wealth;
> he doesn't know that poverty will come to him.
>
> Proverbs 28:22 (CSB)

Before the Industrial Revolution in the late 1700s, making cloth was very expensive. Hours and hours of hand labor were required. Smooth cloth was much more expensive than rough cloth, because spinning fine thread took much longer and weaving more threads per inch was much more work. Thus, if moths ate your clothes, it was a major loss.

Today, moths are less of a threat. What makes a closet full of beautiful clothes worthless? "I wouldn't be caught dead in those old things." "That dress is so out of style." "Nobody wears lapels like that anymore." "Those twenty extra pounds make it hard to get into those slacks." If I can't zip it up, those jeans are worthless.

Similarly, prior to the Industrial Revolution, metal working was difficult, requiring highly skilled labor. Iron, in particular, requires high temperatures to refine and to fashion into tools. Thus, if a metal tool rusted or corroded, it was a major loss.

Today, Americans have many big toys. What makes them worthless? "I can't remember when the RV was last on the road." "I haven't been out in the boat in over a year." A boat that never gets wet is worthless. When I never have time to enjoy my big toys, they are worthless.

In ancient times, security was poor and thieves were common. Mud bricks were not hard to dig through. If thieves stole one's treasures, it was a major loss.

Today, home security is still a problem and modern society has other kinds of thieves. "That used car salesman sold me a lemon." "My stockbroker just wasted my retirement nest egg." "Someone stole my credit card number." "An identity thief emptied my bank account." I can't use treasures that get stolen.

Practically all Americans are rich compared to the majority of mankind. Even those on welfare have a more comfortable lifestyle than most of the world. Paul gave this advice to Timothy for those who do have financial resources.

> Instruct those who are rich in the present age not to be arrogant or to set their hope on the uncertainty of wealth, but on God, who richly provides us with all things to enjoy. Instruct them to do what is good, to be rich in good works, to be generous and willing to share, storing up treasure for themselves as a good foundation for the coming age, so that they may take hold of what is truly life.
>
> 1 Timothy 6:17–19 (CSB)

Even though a friend's church had over a thousand members, she would send a get-well card to anyone in the congregation who was sick. She was always generous and compassionate. She was rich in good works.

The attitudes, actions, and lifestyle described in these verses to Timothy are the way to have treasures in the Kingdom of Heaven. As an American in a profession that pays well, I am in the category of having financial resources, so Paul's advice to Timothy is my template for life. Those who happen to have resources must not be arrogant but must be generous.

Jesus pointed out that the expensive things in daily life are vulnerable. Earth is not a secure place to store treasures. When fashions change, toys lay idle, and the stock market tanks, modern treasures are not worth much.

What can I store in heaven? What kind of treasures are there? Paul told Timothy good works result in treasure in heaven. God is a trustworthy banker. If I will live in the Kingdom of Heaven, my heart will be focused on God's kind of treasure.

The eye. There is a cooking pot in my kitchen cabinet. When the mouth of the pot is open then light shines on the bottom of the pot. When the lid is on the pot then the inside is very dark.

> If we walk in the light as [the Father] himself is in the light, we have fellowship with one another, and the blood of Jesus his Son cleanses us from all sin.
>
> 1 John 1:7 (CSB)

The body is like my pot and the eye is like the mouth of my pot. Jesus explained that when the eye is open and functioning, light is seen. When the eye is not functioning, nothing can be seen. A "good eye" can perceive the value of treasures in heaven, but the "bad eye" only values treasures on earth. Without an awareness of treasure in heaven, one's life is completely blind.

Two masters. I simultaneously worked for two bosses in the same company for a while. It was awkward. I could only work a standard week. Each boss deserved only half of my time. However, the tasks each one assigned me could easily take all of my time. Eventually, we determined I would work for just one of them.

> For of this you can be sure: No ... greedy person—such a person is an idolater—has any inheritance in the kingdom of Christ and of God.
>
> Ephesians 5:5 (NIV)

Who is my master? God? Or money? I can't serve both. My master is the one I love. Love is not just a warm feeling. Love is expressed by serving obediently. The greedy churchgoer who is trying to get rich is not a citizen of the Kingdom of Heaven. A greedy person is an idolater, and thus, has no inheritance in the Kingdom. A citizen of the Kingdom serves God rather than money.

Do not worry

I'm at the stage of life where I'm wondering whether there will be enough for retirement. Calculating retirement finances is hard. Jesus said, "Don't worry." I guess that means I'll have enough to eat and drink, no matter what the price of groceries is, and I'll have enough t-shirts to wear during retirement, too.

Matthew 6:25–34 (CSB)[4]

---

25 Therefore I tell you: Don't worry about your life, what you will eat or what you will drink; or about your body, what you will wear. Isn't life more than food and the body more than clothing? 26 Consider the birds of the sky: They don't sow or reap or gather into barns, yet your heavenly Father feeds them. Aren't you worth more than they? 27 Can any of you add one moment to his lifespan by worrying? 28 And why do you worry about clothes? Observe how the wildflowers of the field grow: They don't labor or spin thread. 29 Yet I tell you that not even Solomon in all his splendor was adorned like one of these. 30 If that's how God clothes the grass of the field, which is here today and thrown into the furnace tomorrow, won't he do much more for you—you of little faith? 31 So don't worry, saying, 'What will we eat?' or 'What will we drink?' or 'What will we wear?' 32 For the Gentiles eagerly seek all these things, and your heavenly Father knows that you need them. 33 But seek first the kingdom of God and his righteousness, and all these things will be provided for you. 34 Therefore don't worry about tomorrow, because tomorrow will worry about itself. Each day has enough trouble of its own.

---

[4]Luke 12:22–31 is a parallel passage.

Jesus pointed out how God cares for the birds and wildflowers which are much less important than the disciples, so his conclusion is don't worry.

> Don't worry about anything, but in everything, through prayer and petition with thanksgiving, present your requests to God. And the peace of God, which surpasses all understanding, will guard your hearts and minds in Christ Jesus.
>
> Philippians 4:6–7 (CSB)

Many things in life are uncertain. Worry doesn't accomplish anything. I will ask my heavenly Father, and he will make sure I have everything I need. He provides for the birds and animals,[5] so he will provide for me, too. My focus should be on the Kingdom. Then I will have the peace of God in my heart and mind. Jesus said, "Don't worry." God will make sure I have enough t-shirts.

> Don't let your beauty consist of outward things like elaborate hairstyles and wearing gold jewelry, but rather what is inside the heart—the imperishable quality of a gentle and quiet spirit, which is of great worth in God's sight.
>
> 1 Peter 3:3–4 (CSB)

Peter gave this advice to Christian wives, including those whose husbands might not be believers. His advice about clothes is applicable to guys, too. Clothes are less important than one's character.

My wife noticed my style was "rumpled." I had not purchased much in the way of business attire. Why would a rumpled guy need a suit? When I realized wearing a suit to work every day was necessary for good relationships on the job, we went shopping. The Lord provided my salary to pay for good quality clothes, and he also gave me a wife who knows bargains when she sees them.

God was the original clothier. After the Fall, he provided clothes for Adam and Eve. He clothes the flowers, too. Wild flowers may not last long, but God makes them beautiful anyway. He will give me the clothes I need, even if my work uniform is a suit.

> Greed should not even be heard of among you, as is proper for saints.
>
> Ephesians 5:3 (CSB)

Advertising is everywhere. "Buy this!" "Buy that!" The news media explains every social phenomenon with economics. The public image of success is having money, cars, houses, big toys, clothes, and so on. Ordinary people spend huge amounts to look prosperous, even if in reality they are deep in debt. People spend their cash on lottery tickets, hoping to get rich quick. Self-help books and "business opportunities" are everywhere. We are surrounded by a society motivated by materialism.

---

[5] Psalm 104:27–28.

Sadly, many Christians chase after wealth just as much as their pagan neighbors. They have not yet put this teaching of Jesus into practice, "Seek first his Kingdom and his righteousness." They don't know that God is our source.

> His divine power has given us everything required for life and godliness through the knowledge of him who called us by his own glory and goodness.
>
>   2 Peter 1:3 (CSB)

An American friend in China invited my wife and me to come for a visit. We knew it was something the Lord wanted us to do, but we didn't have the money to pay for the trip. We made plans anyway, and as the time approached, we received enough money from an unexpected source. God provided what we needed.

Is living the Kingdom lifestyle my first priority? Or is my mind occupied with anxiety about achieving an American lifestyle? Jesus promised if the Kingdom of Heaven and righteousness have first place, then God will take care of providing things like food and clothing. My loving heavenly Father knows what I need and gives me everything required to live a godly life.

Do not judge

We were in the stands watching the home team's football game. The quarterback threw the ball downfield, just beyond the fingertips of the receiver. The crowd yelled, "That quarterback can't hit the broadside of a barn." "That receiver can't catch anything." Then I thought about what would happen if I was the quarterback or the receiver.

Matthew 7:1–5 (CSB)[6]

---

1 Do not judge, so that you won't be judged. 2 For you will be judged by the same standard with which you judge others, and you will be measured by the same measure you use. 3 Why do you look at the splinter in your brother's eye but don't notice the beam of wood in your own eye? 4 Or how can you say to your brother, 'Let me take the splinter out of your eye,' and look, there's a beam of wood in your own eye? 5 Hypocrite! First take the beam of wood out of your eye, and then you will see clearly to take the splinter out of your brother's eye.

In English, the word *judge* has a wide range of meaning: recognize, discern, assess, evaluate, adjudicate, condemn, and many more. The Greek word for *judge*[7] similarly has a wide range of meanings. The illustration of a splinter

---

[6]Luke 6:41–42 is a parallel passage.
[7]The Greek word *krino* (*Strong's* No. 2919).

in the eye indicates that in this passage, *judge* means to find faults in another person.

> At the same time, [young widows] also learn to be idle, going from house to house; they are not only idle, but are also gossips and busybodies, saying things they shouldn't say.
>
> 1 Timothy 5:13 (CSB)

Many people are looking for solutions to personal problems. That is why they buy so many self-help and pop-psychology books. The real solution to such personal problems is a relationship with the living God who forgives sin and resurrects broken lives.

Some people think their mission in life is to be a psychiatrist to those around them. Such a person is always interested in fixing my thought life, social life, and sex life. But like a "log in the eye," the neighborhood psychiatrist has unresolved personal problems just like everyone else.

I may have read all the pop-psychology books and seen all the videos, but that is no excuse for me to be a busybody. Even though it may be true Mr. So-and-so has faults, I should not be spreading gossip. Whatever criteria I use when fault-finding will be equally applied to me. I am not above God's standard of righteousness and justice. However, there is a godly way to give help to others.

> Brothers and sisters, if someone is overtaken in any wrongdoing, you who are spiritual, restore such a person with a gentle spirit, watching out for yourselves so that you also won't be tempted. Carry one another's burdens; in this way you will fulfill the law of Christ.
>
> Galatians 6:1–2 (CSB)

My wife had a couple of cute dishes on the wall which her mother had given her. I accidentally knocked one off and broke it. She was mad at me for being so clumsy, but she forgave me.

Being generous and merciful does not mean I can't recognize sin, human frailty, and mistakes. When I do see faults, I can respond with grace and forgiveness, instead of bitterness, retaliation, and condemnation. Jesus taught that I am to imitate God's forgiveness and mercy.[8] If I show abundant mercy regarding the faults of others, then I will receive mercy.

Responding with grace to the faults of others is much easier if I have already experienced the Father's forgiveness for my faults. Even though I clearly see my own human frailty, I know God loves me. Kingdom living is abiding in his continuous grace and extending grace to those around me.

---

[8] 5:7 and 6:14–15.

Do not give what is holy to dogs

My father told me, "You don't have to tell everything you know to everybody all the time." He had encountered unscrupulous businessmen in his career. He taught me to use discretion when dealing with people.

Matthew 7:6 (CSB)

---

6 Don't give what is holy to dogs or toss your pearls before pigs, or they will trample them under their feet, turn, and tear you to pieces.

Wild dogs and wild pigs only care about what they eat. They are completely selfish. Some people fit this metaphor.

Act wisely toward outsiders, making the most of the time. Let your speech always be gracious, seasoned with salt, so that you may know how you should answer each person.
Colossians 4:5–6 (CSB)

Some people can't be trusted to respect precious things, precious thoughts, precious beliefs, and precious relationships. Secular people do not understand nor respect many elements of Kingdom living.[9] They are like the pagan outsiders in biblical times.

Some things in the Kingdom are sacred. Some experiences are precious to me like pearls. I don't have to talk about those things with people who will attack me for them. I can relate to them on a superficial level with my guard up.

Priorities in the Kingdom

Jesus revealed priorities in the Kingdom of Heaven by rejecting the world's patterns. Will I trust God with my future, or will I use all the world's strategies to assure a comfortable future? Jesus warned about four dangers of the world's patterns. I will reject the way the world lives and embrace Kingdom living.

Do not serve money. Money can buy clothes and big toys which moths and rust ruin. Home security is just as much a problem today as in Jesus' day. Treasure in heaven is a much safer investment. The desire for money in the bank blinds one to the value of treasure in heaven. Even if one is a churchgoer, when money is an idol, there is no inheritance in the Kingdom of Heaven. I will serve God instead of money.

---

[9]Ephesians 4:18.

Do not worry. I don't need to worry about the price of groceries. I don't need to worry about having the right work uniform or enough t-shirts. If I focus on the Kingdom, God will provide everything I need to live a godly life.

Do not judge. Reading all the self-help books does not qualify me to be a busybody or a gossip. My fault-finding criteria will be equally applied to me, too. When I see sin and mistakes, I will respond with grace and forgiveness, instead of condemnation.

Do not give what is holy to dogs. Some people will not respect my pearls. I don't have to share precious thoughts, beliefs, and relationships with untrustworthy people who will attack me for them. I will relate to them on a superficial level.

Priorities in the Kingdom. Instead of money, I will serve God. Instead of worry, I will trust the Father's provision for me. Instead of fault-finding, I will extend grace to others. Instead of entrusting precious things to worldly people, I will guard my pearls. These are my priorities in the Kingdom of Heaven.

6

Entering the Kingdom

Sooner or later we shall find out where a man stands...
In such times as these, Jesus requires his disciples to distinguish be-
tween appearance and reality, between themselves and pseudo-Christians.
Dietrich Bonhoeffer[1]

What is the difference between a solid wood cabinet and fake wood? From the outside the wood grain may look the same. When I look closely at the finish, the fake wood has a photo of wood grain glued on the outside. The side panels are particle board, and the edges reveal the top is plywood. Similarly, a close look distinguishes between a genuine Christian and a pseudo-Christian.

Bonhoeffer wrote during the rise of Nazi Germany. At that time, the Nazis were subverting church institutions, so they would support the government. It was important for believers to recognize who was a true disciple and who was a pseudo-Christian. The same is essential today. What is the difference between a true Christian believer and a fake Christian? On judgment day, the pseudo-Christians will say, "Lord, Lord!" but Jesus will say, "I never knew you."[2]

This chapter discusses three passages that all begin with commands. Their common thread is about entering the Kingdom of Heaven.[3]

Ask, seek, and knock

Due to our upcoming move, my wife and I gave some big heavy furniture to Robert. However, he didn't have a truck to move it to his house. He said he would borrow his friend Bill's pickup truck. It did not matter to Bill how Robert asked for help. It could have been by text message, email, voice mail, phone call, or in-person. Bill was glad to help.

---

[1] Bonhoeffer, pp. 213, 214.
[2] 7:21–23 (CSB).
[3] The outline groups the passages in 7:7–23 together, because each one begins with a command.

Matthew 7:7–12 (CSB)[4]

---

7 Ask, and it will be given to you. Seek, and you will find. Knock, and the door will be opened to you. 8 For everyone who asks receives, and the one who seeks finds, and to the one who knocks, the door will be opened. 9 Who among you, if his son asks him for bread, will give him a stone? 10 Or if he asks for a fish, will give him a snake? 11 If you then, who are evil, know how to give good gifts to your children, how much more will your Father in heaven give good things to those who ask him. 12 Therefore, whatever you want others to do for you, do also the same for them, for this is the Law and the Prophets.

The heavenly Father is more generous than human fathers. He is always attentive to our requests.

> The eyes of the Lord are on the righteous
> and his ears are open to their prayer.
> But the face of the Lord is against
> those who do what is evil.
>
> 1 Peter 3:12 (CSB)

Ask, seek, and knock are three ways to make a request.[5] My Father in heaven does not care about the form of the request. He is always ready to respond. I don't need to write a formal signed sealed letter. I don't need to use eloquent language. I don't need a holy man to get God's attention for me. I don't need an army of prayer warriors to vote for my request. I just need to ask my heavenly Father, seek his ways, or knock on his door. It's simple. He has promised to respond.

> How priceless your faithful love is, God!
> People take refuge in the shadow of your wings.
> They are filled from the abundance of your house.
> You let them drink from your refreshing stream.
>
> Psalm 36:7–8 (CSB)

I was about to graduate from college when my father saw my mustache for the first time. Facial hair was not traditional in our family. For a graduation gift, he gave me a tiny comb. To me, it symbolized his acceptance of my mustache. Parents know how to give good gifts to their children.

God has so many blessings he gives to his children that he must have a warehouse somewhere.[6] His blessings are like a buffet banquet table packed with delicious food and refreshing drinks. My Father in heaven is generous. He loves his children. He gives them good gifts.[7] He responds to their requests.

---

[4]Luke 11:9–13 and Luke 6:31 are parallel passages.
[5]Philippians 4:6–7.
[6]Psalm 31:19.
[7]Psalm 103:2–5.

The Father's generous character is the guarantee he will answer. Because my heavenly Father is generous, I should be too.

> So it is sin to know the good and yet not do it.
>
> James 4:17 (CSB)

A couple of kids rang my doorbell. I whispered a quick prayer as I answered the door. They were raising money for the high school band. They were surprised when I took the time to visit with them for a few minutes. At the end, I made a contribution. Each time someone comes to my door, I pray for the Lord to show me how to respond.

Because my heavenly Father is generous, it is not sufficient in the Kingdom just to do no harm. Not doing good that I ought to do is sin. I must be proactive to do good. Knowing what is good is not hard most of the time. "Whatever you want others to do for you" is an easy guide.[8] God prepares good works for me to do.[9] Doing good is expected of citizens of the Kingdom.

Enter through the narrow gate

I was driving along on a nice wide four-lane divided highway out in the country. A small sign by a narrow ramp said, "All traffic exit here." I wondered why I should exit when the road ahead looked so good. As I went around the curve on the ramp, I saw the highway ended over the next hill.

Matthew 7:13–14 (CSB)

---

13 Enter through the narrow gate. For the gate is wide and the road broad that leads to destruction, and there are many who go through it. 14 How narrow is the gate and difficult the road that leads to life, and few find it.

These two verses present a choice as a metaphor. Will one choose an attractive gate and a convenient road? Or will one choose a narrow gate and a road with persecution?[10] The choice has eternal consequences, destruction or life.

Nicodemus visited Jesus one night. Jesus explained to him who can enter the Kingdom of Heaven.

> Jesus replied, "Truly I tell you, unless someone is born again, he cannot see the kingdom of God."
>
> "How can anyone be born when he is old?" Nicodemus asked him. "Can he enter his mother's womb a second time and be born?"

---

[8] A negative form of the Golden Rule is an ancient ethical teaching. Jesus expressed it as a positive command (Carson, p. 187).

[9] Ephesians 2:10.

[10] Carson, pp. 188–189.

> Jesus answered, "Truly I tell you, unless someone is born of water and the Spirit, he cannot enter the kingdom of God."
>
> John 3:3–5 (CSB)

I have been born naturally[11] and I have been born by the Holy Spirit to new life. That means I am allowed to see the Kingdom and to enter the Kingdom.

The wide gate is easy to enter, because it seems everyone else is entering there. The broad road is paved with selfishness, greed, and immorality.[12] It's easy to imitate everyone else, but the broad road leads to destruction. The consequences are eternal.

The narrow gate is not entered by going to church on Christmas and Easter. The narrow gate is not entered by getting a seminary or Bible school education.[13] The narrow gate is not entered by membership in some exclusive church. The difficult road is not marked with dos and don'ts. The difficult road is marked by the footsteps of Jesus. "Follow me." Walking the difficult road is sustained by an intimate relationship with the Father. The rewards are eternal.

Beware of false prophets

In the 1980s, the news media reported that a prominent Christian televangelist had fallen into sexual immorality. Not long after, the public learned another had fallen into financial misconduct. They may have tried to hide their sins, but God's love for them and for his people wouldn't let sin fester and poison.

Matthew 7:15–23 (CSB)

---

15 Be on your guard against false prophets who come to you in sheep's clothing but inwardly are ravaging wolves. 16 You'll recognize them by their fruit. Are grapes gathered from thornbushes or figs from thistles? 17 In the same way, every good tree produces good fruit, but a bad tree produces bad fruit. 18 A good tree can't produce bad fruit; neither can a bad tree produce good fruit. 19 Every tree that doesn't produce good fruit is cut down and thrown into the fire. 20 So you'll recognize them by their fruit.

21 Not everyone who says to me, 'Lord, Lord,' will enter the kingdom of heaven, but only the one who does the will of my Father in heaven. 22 On that day many will say to me, 'Lord, Lord, didn't we prophesy in your name, drive out demons in your name, and do many miracles in your name?' 23 Then I will announce to them, 'I never knew you. Depart from me, you lawbreakers!'

---

[11] *Water* in John 3:5 refers to when a mothers' water breaks during birth.

[12] 1 Corinthians 6:9–11; Galatians 5:19–21; and Ephesians 5:5.

[13] Even though education can be valuable in this life, it is not a substitute for a relationship with God.

In the Bible, a *prophet* was simply someone who was God's spokesman for an occasion. His role was not limited to foretelling the future. *Prophet* was not necessarily the person's main job title. I appreciate the many godly men and women who have spoken the word of God I needed at just the right time. However, some who claim to hear from God are not correct or have impure motives.

> There were indeed false prophets among the people, just as there will be false teachers among you. They will bring in destructive heresies, even denying the Master who bought them, and will bring swift destruction on themselves.
>
> 2 Peter 2:1 (CSB)

Jesus is the Good Shepherd, and the citizens of the Kingdom are like his sheep. He is protective of his sheep. A wolf may look like everyone else, but actually is seeking to exploit the sheep.

In some churches, Bible teachers are highly respected.[14] A false teacher may sound good, but immoral actions will corrupt the flock more than false words. Jesus warned his sheep to be careful who they emulate.

In some churches, the gift of prophecy[15] is important. Someone who is recognized as a so-called prophet will come to town, giving a personal prophecy to everyone who asks for one. Some speak true words from God, but others speak from their own mind. Jesus warned his sheep to be careful who they listen to.

> Dear friends, do not believe every spirit, but test the spirits to see if they are from God, because many false prophets have gone out into the world.
>
> 1 John 4:1 (CSB)

I have two mango trees in my back yard. It is hard to tell when the fruit is ripe or rotten. When a mango falls to the ground, I look it over. Is it too green? Is it hard? Does it have rotten spots? Did a squirrel eat a bite? If it looks okay, I bring it in the house for final ripening. After a day or two, I get the proof when I cut into it.

Some Christians only look at external credentials, reputation, or flamboyant style. They can be gullible. Jesus explained how to differentiate true teachers and prophets from false ones. Examine their "fruit."

The first kind of fruit is the effect teaching or prophecy has on the listeners. Does it build faith and godliness or does it make people think they can manipulate God? Does it bring fear or cultivate greed? Does the prophecy promise get-rich-quick results? Such teaching or prophecy comes from the flesh.

A second kind of fruit is the Fruit of the Spirit[16] in the personal life of the teacher or prophet. How can someone hear from God when worldly habits and

---

[14]James 3:1.
[15]1 Corinthians 12:10.
[16]Galatians 5:22–23.

patterns characterize one's personal life? It is hard to know about the personal life of a traveling minister. This kind of fruit inspection is possible when the teacher or prophet lives among the sheep.

> The one who says, "I have come to know [Jesus]," and yet doesn't keep his commands, is a liar, and the truth is not in him.
> 1 John 2:4 (CSB)

In the 1990s, a preacher with a national reputation visited my church, teaching about faith and healing. Many people were healed in the services. He extended his visit to about a month of special meetings. A short time later, we learned that he had had an affair, and that he and his wife had divorced. Sin made that time a dark chapter in his life, even though the special meetings were extraordinary.

Christian people and pastors are sometimes awed by the apparent spiritual gifts of a visiting preacher. They think spiritual gifts validate a person as God's spokesman. Likewise, false teachers and prophets don't know they are false. They think they are okay. No matter how confident the visitor is, extraordinary works of spiritual power are not what Jesus is looking for. Prophecy, exorcism, or even miracles are not evidence of God's approval. Jesus will say, "I never knew you," to a false teacher.

Who has God's approval? "The one who does the will of my Father in heaven."[17] What is his will? Jesus taught us what God wants, namely, living the Kingdom lifestyle.

Entering the Kingdom

The Kingdom of Heaven sounds like a nice way to live. How can I get started living the Kingdom lifestyle? How can one enter the Kingdom? Jesus said to do three things: ask the Father, enter the narrow gate, and beware of false prophets.

Ask, seek, and knock. Jesus told me to reach out to my heavenly Father. Entering the Kingdom means establishing a relationship with the Father. He wants me to ask for what I need, to search for his ways, and to knock on his door. He will answer; I will find; and our relationship will be open. His generous character is the guarantee he will answer. I must be generous with others like he is toward me.

Enter through the narrow gate. Jesus confronted me with the call to follow him. Entering the Kingdom is a choice. Will I just go with everyone else, or will I follow Jesus? Following Jesus may not be popular and there may be persecution along the way, but it leads to life.

---

[17]7:21 (CSB).

Beware of false prophets. Jesus warned me about false prophets. The apostle Peter extended his warning to false teachers. Entering the Kingdom means being careful who I emulate and who I listen to. False teachers and false prophets may think they are working for God. They may prophesy, cast out demons, or even perform miracles, but Jesus will say, "I never knew you." Jesus wants obedience from the heart.

Entering the Kingdom. I am reaching out to the heavenly Father. Jesus told Nicodemus being born by the Holy Spirit is necessary to enter the Kingdom of Heaven. I have made my choice. When I repented and invited the Lord to come into my life, the Holy Spirit began my new life. Jesus is my king. My heart and life are his domain. I won't pay attention to false teachers. I am looking for Jesus to return when his Kingdom will cover the whole world. I am a citizen of the Kingdom of Heaven.

7

Living in the Kingdom

[Jesus] does not allow his hearers to go away and make of his sayings what they will picking and choosing from them whatever they find helpful, and testing them to see if they work...

The only proper response to this word which Jesus brings with him from eternity is simply to do it.

Dietrich Bonhoeffer[1]

Many Christians say the Sermon on the Mount is their favorite passage. They say it teaches good ethics and Christian values. They can even quote a few famous verses that sounded nice.

When I go to the grocery store, I carefully select which fruits to buy. I only buy my favorite kinds. I carefully inspect each one. I avoid those that are bruised or too ripe.

Following Jesus is different than shopping at the grocery store. Following Jesus means I let him bring his word to me. I can't pick which word is my favorite. I can't say whether I like applying it to my life. I must simply obey.

Two builders

In 2017, Hurricane Harvey devastated metropolitan Houston, Texas, with huge amounts of rain. Peggy's home was safe on high ground, but all the roads out of her neighborhood were flooded. Homes in flooded areas were washed away or ruined.

Matthew 7:24–27 (CSB)[2]

---

24 Therefore, everyone who hears these words of mine and acts on them will be like a wise man who built his house on the rock.

---

[1] Bonhoeffer, pp. 218, 219.
[2] Luke 6:47–49 is a parallel passage.

25 The rain fell, the rivers rose, and the winds blew and pounded that house. Yet it didn't collapse, because its foundation was on the rock. 26 But everyone who hears these words of mine and doesn't act on them will be like a foolish man who built his house on the sand. 27 The rain fell, the rivers rose, the winds blew and pounded that house, and it collapsed. It collapsed with a great crash.

Jesus told a parable of two home builders, one wise and one foolish. Jesus began this parable with *therefore*, so this parable applies to all the teaching of the Sermon on the Mount.

When rain and floods came, the ground under the foolish builder's house was washed away. Walls cracked and storm winds blew against the fragile house. Eventually it fell.

Jesus said people who hear his words, Kingdom teaching, but do not put them in to practice, Kingdom living, are like that foolish builder. When the storms of life come, their lives will fall apart.

Churchgoers claim to be Christians. They listen to sermons on Sunday, but many do not put Kingdom teaching into practice on Monday. In some churches, even the Sunday sermon lacks Kingdom teaching. If churchgoers don't live the Kingdom lifestyle, their lives will lack a solid foundation. Circumstances will push them around from one crisis to another.

The wise builder was different. The foundation of his house was a rock that could not be washed away.

> Teach me, Lord, the meaning of your statutes,
> and I will always keep them.
> Help me understand your instruction,
> and I will obey it
> and follow it with all my heart.
> Help me stay on the path of your commands,
> for I take pleasure in it.
>
> Psalm 119:33–35 (CSB)

The wise builder experienced the same storms as the foolish builder. Storms come to everyone. Citizenship in the Kingdom is not a ticket to avoid hardship. However, the wise builder's house was built on a rock, and thus, was able to withstand the storm.

A citizen of the Kingdom has a life whose foundation is Jesus and his teaching. The Kingdom life has an intimate relationship with the Father. His resources are available, because he loves his children. Listening to sermons on Sunday is good, but living the Kingdom lifestyle on Monday is better.

Living in the Kingdom

In the Sermon on the Mount, Jesus portrayed living in the Kingdom of Heaven in several dimensions. What are the citizens of the Kingdom like? Is legalistic obedience required? How should religious good works be done? What are priorities for Kingdom living? How can one enter the Kingdom of Heaven?

Citizens of the Kingdom. The citizens of the Kingdom have hearts that reflect the character of Jesus. Consequently, they have the Kingdom and are blessed by God in other ways. As a community of faith, they are like salt in society. Their good works are so obvious they are like a city on a hill. Living in the Kingdom of Heaven means my attitude will be the same as the attitude of Jesus.

Law in the Kingdom. Jesus fulfilled the Old Testament Law. The Pharisees thought legalism would please God, but it is insufficient. Jesus illustrated how obedience comes from the heart. Murder, sexual immorality, the damage of divorce, the arrogance of oaths, lust for revenge, and hatred for enemies all flow from the heart. Living in the Kingdom of Heaven means obeying from a faithful heart, so the Law's purpose is fulfilled.

Religion in the Kingdom. Giving to the poor, praying, and fasting are religious good works which are rewarding. If I do things to impress others with how pious I am, their respect is my reward. But God will reward me if I do them out of love for him. Living in the Kingdom of Heaven means doing religious good works without expecting anyone to notice.

Priorities in the Kingdom. My priorities must conform to the Kingdom rather than the world. I won't serve money. I won't worry. I won't look for the faults of others. I won't entrust precious truths and experiences of the Kingdom to those who will despise them. Instead, I will serve the Lord. I will trust God for my needs. I will extend grace to others. I will guard my spiritual pearls. Living in the Kingdom of Heaven means having different priorities than the world.

Entering the Kingdom. A relationship with my heavenly Father is essential for entering the Kingdom. The invitation to enter the Kingdom means making a choice between Kingdom living and the world's ways. Jesus warned about false prophets and teachers. They may be sincere, but do they know Jesus? As Jesus told Nicodemus, living in the Kingdom of Heaven begins by being born by the Holy Spirit.

Living in the Kingdom. The American Dream includes things like owning your home, a good paying job, a good education for your kids, and so on, irrespective of social class or background. It's not easy. It's a competitive world out there. *Worldly success* is defined as becoming prosperous and respected in the community. But in the Kingdom, success means loving my enemy, doing good from the heart, and serving others more than myself.

The crowd may have gathered on the hillside to see a miracle worker, but he taught them with authority about the Kingdom of Heaven.

Matthew 7:28–29 (CSB)

---

28 When Jesus had finished saying these things, the crowds were astonished at his teaching, 29 because he was teaching them like one who had authority, and not like their scribes.

Jesus confronts me with a choice. Will I focus my attention, time, and energy on achieving worldly success? Or will I consistently pursue a Kingdom lifestyle? If I am wise, I'll build my life on the Rock—Jesus himself.[3]

---

[3] 1 Peter 2:4–6.

Part II

Apostles of the Kingdom

8

Commission

Jesus imparts to [the apostles] a share in the highest gift he possesses, his power over unclean spirits, and over the devil who has taken possession of the human race.

Dietrich Bonhoeffer[1]

An apprentice learns his trade by watching a master and then doing the same thing. It usually takes some practice, but the master is there to give direction and encouragement. The apprentice starts with simple tasks. He increases his knowledge and skill step by step until he is qualified to work on his own, doing the same things the master does. The disciples were like apprentices and Jesus was the master.

Matthew 10:1–5 (CSB)[2]

---

1 Summoning his twelve disciples, he gave them authority over unclean spirits, to drive them out and to heal every disease and sickness.

2 These are the names of the twelve apostles: First, Simon, who is called Peter, and Andrew his brother; James the son of Zebedee, and John his brother; 3 Philip and Bartholomew; Thomas and Matthew the tax collector; James the son of Alphaeus, and Thaddaeus; 4 Simon the Zealot, and Judas Iscariot, who also betrayed him.

5 Jesus sent out these twelve after giving them instructions: . . .

This discourse consists of instructions to the Twelve who were sent on a mission. Jesus had been going from village to village, teaching about the Kingdom and doing works of power which validated his message. Jesus sent the

---

[1] Bonhoeffer, pp. 226–227.
[2] Luke 9:1–2, Mark 3:16–19, Luke 6:13–16, and Acts 1:13 are parallel passages.

twelve disciples out to do what they had seen him do, using the authority he gave them. They were extensions of him.

Jesus' instructions have application for today. All Christians have a part in making disciples.[3] How am I similar to the disciples? What does Jesus ask me to do? What will be my response to this word?

This chapter examines the commission Jesus gave the Twelve. He told the apostles what to do. He expected them to do what they had observed him doing, works of power. These were works of compassion, helping people who were suffering.

Where to go

My pastor took a mission trip to Haiti. After seeing the desperate needs and the opportunities for the gospel, he wanted to resign as a pastor in America and become a missionary to Haiti. The Lord prevented him from doing so, but instead, over the years, his church sent out many others as missionaries, including his own son.

Matthew 10:5–6 (CSB)

---

5 Don't take the road that leads to the Gentiles, and don't enter any Samaritan town. 6 Instead, go to the lost sheep of the house of Israel.

Jesus told the apostles where to go on this mission trip. At this time, Jesus was preaching only in Jewish towns and villages. He sent the Twelve out as extensions of what he was doing. After the resurrection, he gave them the Great Commission which broadened their mission field to the whole world.

Jesus came near and said to them, "All authority has been given to me in heaven and on earth. Go, therefore, and make disciples of all nations, baptizing them in the name of the Father and of the Son and of the Holy Spirit, teaching them to observe everything I have commanded you. And remember, I am with you always, to the end of the age."

Matthew 28:18–20 (CSB)

Sometimes God sends one far from home. Several of my friends have become permanent residents of other countries, because God sent them there. I have never been sent by a denomination to a mission field, but my wife and I made several trips to visit Christian friends overseas. I taught Bible studies while there. I also made some business trips to far away places. When I got there, I often found believers with whom to fellowship.

---

[3] 28:18–20.

Sometimes the most fruitful mission field is nearby. My wife and I have had many Bible studies in our home and other local homes. Home has been our place for making disciples.

When I went off to college, I promptly joined a local church near the campus. After a short while, I realized many in the congregation did not believe the Bible. That group became my mission field. During my years there, I saw some grow in their fidelity to God's Word. On the outside, they looked like solid church people, but on the inside, they were like lost sheep.

Kingdom obedience means I will go where God says to go and I will not go where he has not sent me. His place for me could be far away or close to home.

What to say

While we were visiting China, a college student invited my wife and me to an underground church meeting that evening. This was not on our agenda. Even though it could be dangerous, we took a taxi with him to an apartment where about twenty people crowded into the living room. Then they asked us to share from the Bible. I had not prepared a Bible study, but I had meditated on a few verses that morning. So, I shared a few thoughts, and in the ensuing discussion, they responded. We had no plans to go there. We didn't prepare a sermon. We didn't know what to do, but God arranged it all.

Matthew 10:7 (CSB)

---

7 As you go, proclaim: 'The kingdom of heaven has come near.'

Jesus told the apostles what to say. Their message was the same as what Jesus was preaching at this time,[4] which was also the same as what John the Baptist had recently preached.[5] The apostles were an extension of Jesus' ministry.

I have the gospel message in me, too. Because I have embraced the gospel, I can speak from experience.

> The message is near you, in your mouth and in your heart. This is the message of faith that we proclaim: If you confess with your mouth, "Jesus is Lord," and believe in your heart that God raised him from the dead, you will be saved.
>
> Romans 10:8–9 (CSB)

When one realizes the Kingdom of Heaven is near, the logical thing to do is to repent, because judgment day is almost here. The Kingdom also offers a

---

[4] 4:17.
[5] 3:2.

wonderful life here in this world and then eternal life. Announcing the Kingdom of Heaven is near is a call for action.

My wife and I stayed at a hotel in Toronto. In the evening, it sounded like airplanes were flying down the hall of the hotel. It was obvious we were near the airport.

The word *near* has several meanings: near in space, near in time, and near in relationships. During Jesus' earthly ministry, the Kingdom was near in space, because Jesus himself was nearby. The Kingdom is wherever the king is. The Kingdom is near in space to believers today because the Holy Spirit is inside the believer. Believers today carry the Kingdom with them everywhere they go. Sometimes people notice a change in the atmosphere when a believer comes in the room.

The Kingdom was near in time for the disciples, because soon Jesus would be resurrected from the dead. The cross and resurrection established the Kingdom of Heaven here on earth. The Kingdom is near in time for an unbeliever. The Kingdom's arrival is just a moment past repentance. The message of faith says "Jesus is Lord," because his resurrection really happened. The Kingdom is near in time if one will repent and believe. Believers are waiting expectantly for the return of Jesus when his reign will be established on earth. The consummation of the Kingdom is near in time. It can happen at any moment. Human time scales are not important to God.

The Kingdom was near in relationship with Jesus for the Twelve. They spent all their time together. The Kingdom is near in relationship with God for believers. Life in the Kingdom is based on an intimate relationship with the Father. The closer I get in my relationship with him, more near the Kingdom is in my life. The cross and resurrection made a way for me to receive forgiveness for my sins. The barrier between me and the Kingdom was removed. The Kingdom is near in relationship.

The Kingdom is near to me in space, in time, and in relationship with God. I will respond to this announcement with repentance and faith.

What to do

I took a religious studies course in college. The students debated with each other whether the theology of Karl Barth or Paul Tillich was better. They were unaware that getting prayers answered is more important than a favorite theologian.

Matthew 10:8 (CSB)[6]

---

8 Heal the sick, raise the dead, cleanse those with leprosy, drive out demons. Freely you received, freely give.

---

[6]10:8 is the theme of the following chapter: Edward B. Allen, Chapter 13, "Speak softly and carry a big stick," *Love, Sex, Money, and Power*, pp. 105–114.

Jesus gave the apostles authority to heal every kind of sickness and to drive demons out of people. The Kingdom message is more than philosophical sermons. Works of power are an essential part of the Kingdom message.

> For the kingdom of God is not a matter of talk but of power.
>
> 1 Corinthians 4:20 (CSB)

Today, we hear reports of miracles in primitive desperate circumstances where modern medicine is not available and where no one excuses demonic activity as mental illness. In primitive circumstances, scientific documentation of miracles is not available, so skeptics doubt their validity. However, those who are healed are thankful for what God has done.

Christians in America wonder why we don't see more works of power. There are various reasons. Modern society is hostile to the Kingdom message. Faith is despised.[7] Skeptics demand documented proof God is alive. People look for human solutions to life's problems instead of God's solutions, and so on.

Preaching "the Kingdom of Heaven is near" is linked to works of power which validate the message.[8] Too often modern churches don't hear the message preached. Too often ordinary Christians are not telling the message to their friends and neighbors. When there is no message, there is no need for validating works of power.

God has not changed. He still wants the Kingdom message to be preached and to be validated by works of power.

Heal the sick. After his sermon, a visiting preacher invited the people to come for prayer for healing. He went down the line across the front of the church, praying for each person. From across the room, I heard a scream and some cracking noises. The host pastor's teenage daughter had such severe scoliosis (curvature of the spine) that she could not participate in sports. After prayer, her spine straightened out while her parents watched. Later that week, her doctor confirmed she was healed and gave her permission to play any sport she wanted.

When Jesus healed, someone's faith was usually tested. Sometimes it was the disciples, sometimes the victim of the sickness, sometimes a parent, and sometimes a friend. Faith is an important part of healing the sick.[9] Sometimes healing comes first to get someone's attention, and then faith in the Kingdom message follows. Sometimes the Kingdom message is explained and healing follows.

I am thankful to God for all the natural mechanisms by which people get healed and for the wisdom of modern medicine. Someone has said, "Doctors treat, but God heals." Sometimes healing is through natural processes which God created. Sometimes God's wisdom is instrumental. Sometimes Spirit-led

---

[7]Mark 6:1–6.
[8]Bonhoeffer, p. 230.
[9]James 5:15.

advice is the key. Sometimes healing is miraculous. No matter how someone is healed, I praise God.

I will pray for healing of anyone when asked. I am especially eager to pray for healing when doctors don't know what to do or have given up hope. In desperate circumstances, God's mercy is most obvious and he gets the credit. When I pray for others, I don't try to figure out who has faith, or who will be healed and who may die. I just pray in faith. The results are God's business. He sees the hearts and faith of everyone involved in each situation. He redeems each situation in his own way. The Kingdom message is proclaimed through prayer for the sick. Faith responds. Healing validates the message.

Raise the dead. Lauri's son was about fifteen months old when he got chicken pox. When his fever spiked, he had a grand mal seizure. She put him in cool bath water and started praying. He quit breathing and turned blue. Because Lauri knew God gave her authority, she commanded her son's spirit to come back into his body. Then he took a gasping breath. He fully recovered.

Jesus gave the apostles authority to raise the dead. When someone is raised from the dead, documentation he was clinically dead is not important. Someone may be raised from the dead or healed from a disease at death's doorstep; God gets the glory either way. Often, we'll never know the scientific details. I will pray anyway, and the Kingdom message will be validated.

We know everyone dies eventually. It is a natural part of God's creation, so it is not my job to raise everyone from the dead, just those the Holy Spirit tells me to.[10] I have never had occasion to raise anyone from the dead, but the power of the Holy Spirit in me is sufficient, so I'm ready. The Kingdom message is proclaimed through prayer for raising the dead. Faith responds. Resurrection validates the message.

Cleanse the leper.[11] A friend became addicted to pornography and drugs at a young age and was rejected by his family. Some years later, he had an encounter with God who took away his desire for drugs and destructive behavior. God sent him a mentor who taught him from the Bible and connected him with a local church who embraced him. His life was cleaned up.

In the Jewish culture of Jesus' day, skin disease was a reason afflicted individuals were excluded from society and had to live in separate communities. They were considered unclean. If someone was healed of his skin disease, then the local priest would inspect him to certify he was now clean. He was then allowed to rejoin society. Jesus told the apostles to "cleanse" such people. They would then be freed from their isolation. Jesus' command is applicable to freeing anyone in social isolation.

---

[10]The person who is raised from the dead will die a natural death eventually. After the return of Jesus, believers will all be raised with transformed bodies for eternal life (1 Corinthians 15:51–57).

[11]The Greek word *lepros* (*Strong's* No. 3015), translated *leprosy* in the KJV and CSB, refers to a wide variety of skin diseases, including modern leprosy (Hansen's disease).

In modern society, some diseases are so contagious and dangerous the victim needs to be isolated from society in general. Such diseases have social consequences like skin disease did in ancient times. For example, in the 1980s, when AIDS and HIV[12] were not understood, people avoided contact with victims. Research later showed HIV was not as contagious as originally feared. Similarly, before effective drugs were invented in the twentieth century, tuberculosis and polio required isolation of victims.

Following Jesus' instructions, I will pray for healing of people with contagious diseases without fear. When they are healed, medical professionals will verify they are no longer contagious, so they can rejoin society.

There are also non-medical reasons some people are excluded from society, such as drug addiction, deviant behaviors, prisoners, and ex-convicts. Following Jesus' instructions means loving such outcasts so the Kingdom message and the grace of the Father can redeem their lives from destructive isolation. Everyone has the potential for a life changing relationship with Jesus. They can become "clean" and rejoin society.

The Kingdom message is proclaimed through prayer and loving relationships with outcasts. Faith responds. Cleansing validates the message.

Drive out demons. At the end of a home Bible study, I asked if anyone wanted prayer. When my wife and I prayed for one friend, she spoke in an unnatural voice, shook all over, screamed, and fell on the floor. We had commanded a demon to come out. She was delivered from severe timidity, so that a few years later, she became a school teacher.[13]

The Scriptures plainly teach that demons are real. Religions throughout the world also openly acknowledge the work of demons. However, casting out demons[14] is not common among Christians in modern society.

Modern secular society pretends demons don't exist and makes excuses for the behavior of those afflicted. Hollywood movies have dramatized demons, so that casting them out seems like fantasy. Admitting demons are real is not acceptable in polite society. Acknowledging having a demon can make one a social outcast. Many who are afflicted by demons in modern society accept the excuses offered by atheists. Many Christians also deny demons are active today. It is hard to receive Kingdom deliverance while denying the problem.

Jesus told his disciples to cast out demons, as part of their mission, so I should, too. Some Christians are afraid of encountering the power of a demon. They don't realize the Holy Spirit in a Christian is more powerful than any demon. The Holy Spirit is my defense against demons and he is the offensive power to deliver others from demonic influence.

---

[12] Acquired Immune Deficiency Syndrome (AIDS) can be fatal. It is caused by Human Immunodeficiency Virus (HIV).

[13] Edward B. Allen, *Love, Sex, Money, and Power*, p. 110.

[14] The phrase *demon possessed* (KJV) sounds weird to modern ears. The Greek word's meaning is broad. It could be translated *demonized* (United Bible Societies, *Translator Handbook, s.v.* Matthew 4:24). The demon's location (in, on, around, etc.) does not matter. Getting free of demonic oppression is what counts. I use the phrase *cast out* to mean defeating a demon.

"Discerning of spirits" is a gift of the Holy Spirit.[15] He will help me recognize the difference between demonic influence and an ordinary human spirit or an ordinary medical condition. Once I see the true situation, I can apply the Kingdom message and power effectively.

Deliverance from demons is a sign the Kingdom of Heaven has come.[16] The Kingdom message is proclaimed through driving out demons. Faith responds. Freedom for the victim validates the message.

Freely you received, freely give. The apostles had freely received from Jesus, so he instructed them to give to people without charging money.

When Paul visited Corinth the first time,[17] he had the same approach as the twelve apostles, speaking simply and demonstrating the power of God.

> When I came to you, brothers and sisters, announcing the mystery of God to you, I did not come with brilliance of speech or wisdom. I decided to know nothing among you except Jesus Christ and him crucified. I came to you in weakness, in fear, and in much trembling. My speech and my preaching were not with persuasive words of wisdom but with a demonstration of the Spirit's power, so that your faith might not be based on human wisdom but on God's power.
>
> 1 Corinthians 2:1–5 (CSB)

Paul did not try to be like a professional orator. He didn't need to rehearse his sermons so they would sound eloquent. He didn't need to quote the famous philosophers of his day. All he did was preach that salvation, life in the Kingdom, is provided by faith in Jesus who was crucified so our sins can be forgiven. Then God validated the message with works of power.

The message of the apostles was very simple. No big speeches were necessary to get the point across. Intricate logical arguments, like legal briefs, were not necessary to persuade the audience. There were no politician or celebrity endorsements. The apostles proclaimed the simple Kingdom message. The message was validated by demonstrations of the power of God.

When a friend is going through a personal crisis, I will pray for him and God will intervene on his behalf. Answered prayer opens the heart to hear the simple Kingdom message.

One receives much more than the benefit of miracles when one enters the Kingdom. One receives the Kingdom message. One receives forgiveness of sin. One receives the Father's love, and by the way, receives healing, resurrection, cleansing, and deliverance. These experiences build faith and prepare one to proclaim the Kingdom of Heaven is near with works of power validating the message.

---

[15] 1 Corinthians 12:10 (KJV).
[16] 12:28 and Luke 11:20.
[17] Acts 18:1–18.

What to carry

In the early twentieth century, travel by ship allowed one to pack trunks full of stuff you might need on the trip. By the mid-twentieth century, air travel allowed multiple suitcases to be stowed aboard, with ample overhead bins in the cabin for a comfortable flight. By the twenty-first century, the airlines charge extra for suitcases, the planes are crowded, and airport security limits the types of items allowed. Jesus' advice to travel light has become a necessity.

Matthew 10:9–10 (CSB)[18]

---

9 Don't acquire gold, silver, or copper for your money-belts. 10 Don't take a traveling bag for the road, or an extra shirt, sandals, or a staff, for the worker is worthy of his food.

Angie went on a mission trip to Haiti. The conditions were going to be primitive, so she packed carefully. The trip included a medical clinic in a remote mountain village. She slept on a thin mattress in a church storage room open to the elements. The people were generous with what they had. Most of the clothes the group packed were given away by the end of the trip.

> I don't say this out of need, for I have learned to be content in whatever circumstances I find myself. I know both how to make do with little, and I know how to make do with a lot. In any and all circumstances I have learned the secret of being content—whether well fed or hungry, whether in abundance or in need. I am able to do all things through him who strengthens me.
>
> Philippians 4:11–13 (CSB)

When Paul traveled, he sometimes had plenty of money and provisions and sometimes little. Sometimes he worked to earn his living.[19] Sometimes he depended on the generosity of Christians in another city.[20] He had learned to be content no matter the circumstances, because he knew God would take care of him.

Jesus told the apostles what to carry. They had to travel light and depend on the providence of God and the hospitality of the village people. In modern terms, the twelve apostles were not to take money for hotels, luggage, camping equipment, or spare stuff for "just in case." God would provide the connections with hospitable people. When works of power were validating the disciples' Kingdom message, it was natural for the village people who benefited to extend hospitality to the apostles. This is not surprising.

I can always rely on the providence of God. On some trips I must travel light. On other trips, he will send me into hostile territory where I need to be

---

[18]Mark 6:8–11 and Luke 9:3–5; 10:4–12 are parallel passages.
[19]Acts 18:1–3.
[20]Philippians 4:15–16 and 2 Corinthians 11:9.

prepared.[21] Whenever I pack for a trip, I pray over what to take. It is foolish to lug around stuff that will never be used, and it is foolish to ignore the Holy Spirit when he says, "Pack this." Spirit-led packing is an exciting adventure in faith. When walking in the Spirit, any trip can be a missionary journey.

Where to stay

An English acquaintance heard I had an upcoming business trip to England. She insisted my wife and I visit Christian friends of hers. So, arrangements were made to go see total strangers. We had a delightful weekend with a large family who made room for us in their home. As we left, we prayed for a blessing on their family and their church.

Matthew 10:11–13 (CSB)

---

11 When you enter any town or village, find out who is worthy, and stay there until you leave. 12 Greet a household when you enter it, 13 and if the household is worthy, let your peace be on it; but if it is unworthy, let your peace return to you.

The disciples had something important to share with their hosts, namely, their greeting and their peace. Many of the letters of the New Testament begin or end with a blessing of grace and peace such as these last verses of 2 Thessalonians.

May the Lord of peace himself give you peace always in every way. The Lord be with all of you. I, Paul, am writing this greeting with my own hand, which is an authenticating mark in every letter; this is how I write. The grace of our Lord Jesus Christ be with you all.
2 Thessalonians 3:16–18 (CSB)

Jesus told the disciples where to stay when they arrived in a village. A worthy person was someone who embraced the message of the Kingdom of Heaven. Worldly criteria did not apply. They were not to seek the biggest house in town; they were not to find the most influential politician; and they were not to look for the most popular person in the community. Having accepted the hospitality of a worthy person, the disciples were to stay there as long as they were in that village. Jesus warned against shopping for a more comfortable place. When I am traveling, I will follow the example of the twelve apostles. I will prefer the hospitality of someone who embraces the Kingdom message, and not seek the most prestigious and comfortable accommodations.

If the apostles' host was worthy he would have a continuing blessing due to the apostles' peace resting on the household. If the host turned out not to be worthy after all, then the apostles' peace would leave with them.

---

[21]Luke 22:35–37.

As Jesus' representative, it is my job to bless those around me. God backs up that blessing with his power. I've grown accustomed to saying, "God bless you," in a sincere way, instead of just "Goodbye." Essentially, I am praying on the spot for those around me. The Kingdom lifestyle spreads peace on those around me. God backs it up.

When rejected

I visited a suburban church down the street from where I was staying for the summer. The pastor was friendly, but didn't mention the Bible much in his sermon. The service was religious, but without passion. I could tell they would not appreciate the Kingdom of Heaven intruding on their comfortable lives.

Matthew 10:14–15 (CSB)

---

14 If anyone does not welcome you or listen to your words, shake the dust off your feet when you leave that house or town. 15 Truly I tell you, it will be more tolerable on the day of judgment for the land of Sodom and Gomorrah than for that town.

If the gospel message is rejected, I should not assume it is all my fault. People may reject me, because through the gospel message, Jesus is confronting sin and offering a life they don't want.

[Jesus said:] Whoever listens to you listens to me. Whoever rejects you rejects me. And whoever rejects me rejects the one who sent me.

Luke 10:16 (CSB)

By making a comparison, Jesus implied rejection of the Kingdom message is worse than the immorality of Sodom and Gomorrah which were destroyed by fire from the sky.[22] Rejecting the Kingdom message and refusing hospitality to Kingdom messengers is the worst sort of sin, deserving fiery punishment on judgment day. If a group of people in a place is going to be severely judged by God, I'll shake their dust off my feet, too.[23]

Commission

Jesus commissioned the twelve apostles to go do the same things he was doing, namely, preaching about the Kingdom and validating the message with

---

[22]Sodom and Gomorrah were cities in the time of Abraham which were destroyed by God for their gross immorality (Genesis 19:1–29).

[23]Apparently, shaking the dust off your feet was a common custom in Jesus' time, expressing complete dissociation with a place and the people of that place.

healing, resurrection, cleansing, and deliverance from demons. Applying his instructions to my life, I ask the Holy Spirit for guidance. Where should I go? What should I say? What should I do? What should I pack for each trip? Where should I stay and how can I bless my hosts? What should I do if the gospel is rejected?

Where to go. The apostles had specific instructions directing them where to go. They were to go to the same kind of places Jesus was going to. I will obey my Lord like they did. I will go where he tells me and I will not go unless he sends me. He may send me far away or close to home.

What to say. The apostles' message was "The Kingdom is near." I will respond with repentance and faith. The Kingdom is near to me in space, in time, and in relationship. I have the Holy Spirit within me. I am expecting Jesus to return at any moment. I have an intimate relationship with the Father. I will spread the word that the Kingdom of Heaven is near.

What to do. Works of power validate the preaching of the gospel. This was true for the apostles and is true today. Forgiveness of sin and the Father's love are packaged with healing, resurrection, cleansing, and deliverance. Experiencing these builds my faith and prepares me to proclaim the "Kingdom of Heaven is near."

What to carry. The apostles were not to take hotel reservations, luggage, camping equipment, or extras. They had to trust God to provide what they needed. Whenever I travel, Spirit-led packing is an exciting adventure in faith. Any trip may turn out to have a Kingdom purpose.

Where to stay. The apostles were to let their peace rest on a worthy household, which would be blessed after the apostles left. As a citizen of the Kingdom, I get to spread peace on those around me. I pray for blessings on those I encounter, and God backs it up.

When rejected. If the apostles' message was rejected and they were refused hospitality, a community would face fiery punishment on judgment day. If I encounter rejection, I must just move on and disassociate myself from them.

Commission. I will follow the example of the twelve apostles. I will rely on the Holy Spirit to direct me where to go, what to say, and what to do in each situation. When traveling, he will show me what to pack, and I will rely on him to guide me to places to stay. I will not be surprised when the Kingdom message is rejected; I'll just move on.

9

Expect opposition

Jesus and his disciples will be condemned on all sides for undermining family life, and for leading the nation astray; they will be called crazy fanatics and disturbers of the peace.

Dietrich Bonhoeffer[1]

Bonhoeffer saw the institutional church co-opted in Nazi Germany. True disciples were seen as enemies. In the twentieth century, communism tried and failed to eliminate Christianity. In the twenty-first century, extremists cannot tolerate Christians in Islamic society. In modern America, atheists think Christians have no right to speak in public. They insist religion be kept within church walls and out of sight.

This chapter looks at the various kinds of opposition the apostles would encounter. Jesus warned the disciples to expect opposition. Matthew did not tell us what happened when the apostles went out on this mission, but the book of Acts and church history tell us about the opposition the apostles faced after Pentecost and about persecution of believers since then. Today, Christians in many parts of the world face violence and genocide of their communities.

Shrewd and innocent

Phishing is deception via the Internet which tries to gain something valuable from me. I'm generally shrewd enough to recognize the game, but one time I received a message asking me to write back. I thought I knew the person, so I responded. After a few short messages, I received a long email with a sad story asking for financial help. Then I realized this person whom I did not know was phishing for money. I had quickly assumed this person was a friend. I needed to be more shrewd.

---

[1] Bonhoeffer, p. 239.

Matthew 10:16 (CSB)

---

16 Look, I'm sending you out like sheep among wolves. Therefore be as shrewd as serpents and as innocent as doves.

Jesus recognized the hostility the apostles would face. They could easily be victims, just as sheep are easily the prey of wolves. Their defense against hostile people was shrewdness and innocence. The serpent in the Garden of Eden was said to be the most shrewd of the animals. *Shrewdness* in Hebrew is an admirable quality.[2]

> I want you to be wise about what is good, and yet innocent about what is evil.
>
> Romans 16:19 (CSB)

As Paul recommended to the Romans, when I proclaim the Kingdom message, I need to be shrewd and wise regarding good, discerning good from evil. But I must be innocent of evil, not participating in the evil of the culture around me, because I am a citizen of the Kingdom.

Arrested

There are many ways to be "arrested." I may be charged with a crime by the police, subject to a lawsuit, fined by a homeowners' association, charged with a zoning violation, accused of violating some government regulation, or harassed in a multitude of ways. Frivolous lawsuits and untrue accusations to regulatory agencies are expensive to defend against. False reports in the press or social media can be devastating for a career or business and are very difficult to fend off. The devil thinks proclaiming the Kingdom message is a crime.

Matthew 10:17–20 (CSB)

---

17 Beware of them, because they will hand you over to local courts and flog you in their synagogues. 18 You will even be brought before governors and kings because of me, to bear witness to them and to the Gentiles. 19 But when they hand you over, don't worry about how or what you are to speak. For you will be given what to say at that hour, 20 because it isn't you speaking, but the Spirit of your Father is speaking through you.

Jesus advised the apostles to be prudent. He said, "Beware of them,"[3] and "flee to another [town]."[4] Retreat is sometimes a good strategy.

---

[2] The Hebrew word *'arum* (*Strong's* No. 6175) is translated *cunning* in Genesis 3:1 (CSB).
[3] 10:17 (CSB).
[4] 10:23 (CSB).

> Princes have persecuted me without cause,
> but my heart fears only your word.
>
> Psalm 119:161 (CSB)

If I am arrested or harassed by the government, Jesus promised the Holy Spirit will strengthen me. If I get to witness to the authorities, the Spirit will speak through me. I don't have to hire a professional orator to be my spokesman. (However, having the help of someone who knows the law may be a good idea.) Obeying Jesus can be costly. Am I willing to be arrested for the sake of Jesus and the Kingdom message?

Betrayed

Betrayal is often done by "a thousand small cuts" in a family, in a circle of friends, or in the news media for a public figure. The size of the wound doesn't matter. It is the same hatred of Jesus and hatred of the Kingdom motivating them. Hatred is expressed by actions which are sometimes subtle and sometime violent.

Matthew 10:21 (CSB)

---

21 Brother will betray brother to death, and a father his child. Children will rise up against parents and have them put to death.

Jesus predicted not only would the apostles be arrested, but the proclaimers of the Kingdom would be betrayed by those who should love them the most. Betrayal is hard to understand, hard to imagine, and hard to accept. The deception of sin can be stronger than familial love.

> The wicked person schemes against the righteous
> and gnashes his teeth at him.
> The Lord laughs at him
> because he sees that his day is coming.
> The wicked have drawn the sword and strung the bow
> to bring down the poor and needy
> and to slaughter those whose way is upright.
> Their swords will enter their own hearts,
> and their bows will be broken.
>
> Psalm 37:12–15 (CSB)

The Kingdom is a force that divides people, even close family members. Some embrace the Kingdom, and others reject it. I should expect to see division. Heralds of the Kingdom will be hated by those who reject the message. My response must be the same irrespective of the kind of wound, standing firm to the end.

Hated

In January 2012, the administration of Vanderbilt University promulgated an "all-comers" policy for student clubs that forbid clubs from requiring leaders to subscribe to the beliefs of the group.[5] In particular, the all-comers policy forbid selecting members and leaders based on race, gender, sexual orientation, or religion. For example, an atheist could become a leader of a Christian group. Eventually, a dozen faith-based organizations lost campus recognition, and were forced off-campus. In March 2013, Rollins College implemented the same policy as Vanderbilt University.[6] Vanderbilt's all-comers policy is an example of the hostility to the gospel one often sees in academia. This particular case was driven by those with a gay-rights agenda.

Matthew 10:22 (CSB)

---

22 You will be hated by everyone because of my name. But the one who endures to the end will be saved.

Being hated was not surprising for the apostles and should not be for us today. If I identify with Jesus, I may be a target for the world's hatred.

Do not be surprised, brothers and sisters, if the world hates you.
1 John 3:13 (CSB)

Although others have been confronted with obvious vicious hostility, rarely have I felt hatred for being a follower of Jesus. Perhaps I have been shunned, but I didn't realize it as I went about my business. Because I have the peace of God on the inside, it easy for me to forgive minor slights and forget about them. Then I just move on with life.

Dear friends, don't be surprised when the fiery ordeal comes among you to test you as if something unusual were happening to you.
1 Peter 4:12 (CSB)

Because the gospel has had a positive impact on Western Civilization, persecution of righteousness in America is not as overt nor as violent as in some other cultures. However, persecution of Christians has certainly been happening in modern America, especially in the public sphere. Let us consider some examples.

---

[5]Katherine Weber, "Vanderbilt University Religious Groups Lose Recognition," *The Christian Post*, Apr. 24, 2012. Available at https://www.christianpost.com/news/vanderbilt-university-religious-groups-lose-recognition-73807/ (Current March 1, 2019.)

[6]Denise-Marie Ordway, "Rollins College boots student religious group off campus," *Orlando Sentinel*, March 7, 2013. Available at http://articles.orlandosentinel.com/2013-03-07/features/os-rollins-college-boots-religious-group-20130307_1_student-leaders-rollins-college-rollins-president-lewis-duncan (Current March 1, 2019).

A church wanted to build on some property it had bought, but the local zoning board would not give permission. Apparently, no churches were getting permission to build in that county at that time. Hatred of Christians was evident at the zoning board.[7]

In another place, almost any public expression of Christian faith in the community faced loud opposition. Traditional Christmas carols were missing at the shopping mall and were certainly never allowed at a school music concert. A flood of complaints inundated City Hall when there was a Christmas nativity scene at the fire station. Traditional Christian symbols reflecting the history of Western Civilization were not welcome.

When freedom of religion is protected, opponents try to bottle up the gospel within church walls. "Don't let it into the public square." When freedom of speech is protected, they try to drown out Christian witness and discredit it. "Don't listen to him. He's crazy. That was hate speech." A biblically based message is not welcome.

Fleeing

Jesus taught the apostles to be prudent. He knew the Kingdom would not be welcomed in some places. He advised the apostles to move on when faced with persecution.

Matthew 10:23 (CSB)[8]

---

23 When they persecute you in one town, flee to another. For truly I tell you, you will not have gone through the towns of Israel before the Son of Man comes.

When Christian clubs at Vanderbilt University were unsuccessful in retaining campus recognition after extended negotiations, they moved off-campus. Their student members could still meet there, but it was less convenient and may have been more expensive.

But the Jews [in Antioch Pisidia] incited the prominent God-fearing women and the leading men of the city. They stirred up persecution against Paul and Barnabas and expelled them from their district. But Paul and Barnabas shook the dust off their feet against them and went to Iconium.

Acts 13:50–51 (CSB)

---

[7]Eventually, the church sold that property and bought another where another church had already secured permission long ago. However, there still was opposition as construction proceeded. In due course, the church building was completed and the church grew.

[8]Interpreting the phrase *before the Son of Man comes* in verse 23 is difficult, because no one is sure what event Jesus was referring to (Carson, p. 250).

Even though there were some in Antioch Pisidia who welcomed the gospel, when opposition arose, Paul and Barnabus had to move on to the next city.

Similarly today, I should discern whether the Kingdom message is being received, and I should be prudent in the face of rejection. When I recognize persecution arising, I should move on to another place to proclaim the Kingdom message. There is no sense in staying where one is not welcome and where the Kingdom message is rejected.

Slandered

When I was in college, some of my friends didn't understand why I wouldn't get drunk or high at parties. If I was at a party, I drank my coke and tried to find someone to talk with. The world wonders why believers don't enjoy their kind of parties.

Matthew 10:24–25 (CSB)

---

24 A disciple is not above his teacher, or a slave above his master. 25 It is enough for a disciple to become like his teacher and a slave like his master. If they called the head of the house 'Beelzebul,' how much more the members of his household!

Jesus himself was accused of being in league with the devil.[9] He was accused of driving out demons by the power of Satan instead of by the Holy Spirit.[10] It is not surprising when his followers are also slandered.

[The pagans] are surprised that you don't join them in the same flood of wild living—and they slander you.

1 Peter 4:4 (CSB)

The language of the world is often upside down, calling black white, white black, good bad, and bad good. The deception of the world permeates their talk. They wonder why believers don't talk the way they do.

Jesus warned us who are of his household to expect the same kind of slander he received. I am a student of Jesus. I am a servant of Jesus. Therefore, I should expect the world to treat me the way they treated Jesus.

If you are ridiculed for the name of Christ, you are blessed, because the Spirit of glory and of God rests on you.

1 Peter 4:14 (CSB)

---

[9] *Beelzebul* or *Beelzebub* in Jesus' day referred to the prince of demons, Satan (Carson, p. 253).
[10] 12:24.

Some Bible school students went to a night-club district each Saturday night to share about Jesus. They talked to people hanging out on the street. One guy said to Crystal, "I'm going to call you Crispy, because your brains are fried on Jesus." He meant it as an insult, but Crystal was not offended, because she knew it was for the name of Christ.

An insult hurts me only when my pride is wounded. A meek attitude cannot be pulled down by insults, because the meek person already honors and respects everyone else. If my self-esteem is based on human-level things then human-level insults will hurt. If my self-esteem is based on God's love for me, no insult can touch me, because I know the truth deep down in my soul. I am God's child and a citizen of the Kingdom.

Expect opposition

Disciples of Jesus should expect opposition to the Kingdom message. Jesus warned his apostles to be prepared for persecution. It may be more severe in some places than others, but I must be settled in my heart how I will respond when it happens.

Shrewd and innocent. As a disciple of Jesus, I must learn to discern good from evil, to be shrewd, but not to participate in the evil of those around me, innocent.

Arrested. In modern society, there are many ways to get in trouble with the government. If I do get in trouble for the sake of Jesus and the Kingdom message, the Holy Spirit will help me respond to the authorities.

Betrayed. I am resolved to stand firm as a citizen of the Kingdom, even if family members attack or betray me. It is not surprising that proclaiming the Kingdom divides people.

Hated. I will not be surprised when the Kingdom message and Kingdom messenger is hated. Even though Christianity has been a major part of Western Civilization, traditional Christian symbols in public are often attacked.

Fleeing. If I am confronted by vicious hostility for the sake of the Kingdom, I will forgive wounds big and small and just move on with life. I will be prudent when the Kingdom message is rejected or when faced with persecution. When it arises, I will move on to another place to proclaim the Kingdom message.

Slandered. I am a servant of Jesus. Therefore, I should expect the world to slander me the way they did Jesus.

Expect opposition. Being shrewd yet innocent will equip me to face opposition to the Kingdom message. Moving on is advisable when I see opposition developing. I may be arrested, betrayed, hated, and slandered, but I will stand firm.

10

Do not fear

*[The disciples] must not fear men. Men can do them no harm, for the
power of men ceases with the death of the body.*

Dietrich Bonhoeffer[1]

Bonhoeffer understood the dangers believers faced in Nazi Germany. He could
have gone into exile, but he chose to continue to pastor believers in Germany.
He was not afraid of death. He was executed shortly before the end of World
War II.

This chapter discusses why believers should not be afraid, even in the face
of opposition. Each passage says, "Do not fear." In spite of persecution, all will
be revealed eventually. God, the righteous judge, is obviously the one with the
authority to send the wicked to eternal punishment, but people can only kill
the body. Assured of eternal life, a disciple has no reason to fear.

Nothing will be concealed

Some parts of town are dangerous at night. The unsuspecting might get robbed.
If I have to walk there, I'll avoid the shortcut through the alley and take a few
extra steps to stay on a lighted street. I won't be afraid when I walk in the
light.

Matthew 10:26–27 (CSB)[2]

---

26 Therefore, don't be afraid of them, since there is nothing covered
that won't be uncovered and nothing hidden that won't be made
known. 27 What I tell you in the dark, speak in the light. What you
hear in a whisper, proclaim on the housetops.

---

[1] Bonhoeffer, p. 242.
[2] Luke 12:2–3 is a parallel passage.

No matter what slander comes against me, the truth will come out. The omniscient God will make my innocence public and reveal the secrets of my accusers, both in this life and on judgment day.

If I live the Kingdom lifestyle there is no need to keep secrets.[3] The Kingdom message should be spoken in public where everyone can hear. The Kingdom message is not a secret. I won't be afraid to proclaim it.

They cannot kill the soul

In 2015, a 26-year-old gunman killed nine people at Upqua Community College in Oregon.[4] After killing a teacher, he asked students one by one "Are you a Christian?" and "If you're a Christian, stand up." When someone would stand up, he shot and killed them. These victims were genuine martyrs for the faith.

Matthew 10:28 (CSB)

---

28 Don't fear those who kill the body but are not able to kill the soul; rather, fear him who is able to destroy both soul and body in hell.

Respecting the eternal judge who presides over everyone's eternal destiny, heaven or hell, is smart.

The fear of the Lord is the beginning of knowledge.

Proverbs 1:7 (CSB)

My eternal destiny is more important than fearing death. Persecution may go so far as murder. They may kill the body of the Kingdom messenger. Even extreme persecution is not intimidating, because my life is in the hands of my heavenly Father who loves me. I won't be afraid, because eternal life in the Kingdom is more valuable than life on earth.

You are worth more than sparrows

God knows how many hairs are on my head. I've been losing them in recent years. Some of the brown ones are getting replaced by white ones. I wonder if an angel is assigned to keep track of how many hairs I have. I must be keeping him busy.

---

[3] 1 John 1:7.

[4] Dana Ford and Ed Payne, "Oregon shooting: Gunman dead after college rampage," *CNN*, October 2, 2015. Available at https://www.cnn.com/2015/10/01/us/oregon-college-shooting/index.html (Current March 1, 2019).

Matthew 10:29–31 (CSB)

---

29 Aren't two sparrows sold for a penny? Yet not one of them falls to the ground without your Father's consent. 30 But even the hairs of your head have all been counted. 31 So don't be afraid; you are worth more than many sparrows.

The Father in heaven knows the details of what is going on in his creation. He is interested in the many small details of my life. Therefore, he is interested in the big things of my life, too, like whether somebody will kill me for following Jesus.

> Lord, you have searched me and known me.
> You know when I sit down and when I stand up;
> you understand my thoughts from far away.
> You observe my travels and my rest;
> you are aware of all my ways.
> Before a word is on my tongue,
> you know all about it, Lord.
> You have encircled me;
> you have placed your hand on me.
> This wondrous knowledge is beyond me.
> It is lofty; I am unable to reach it.
>
> Psalm 139:1–6 (CSB)

As the psalmist testified, the Lord knows every detail of my life, where I go, what I think, and what I say. He understands me and my situation better than I know myself.

If the Father is watching over me and his grace is sufficient for every situation, then I don't have any excuse for worrying about being arrested and beaten, being betrayed by family, fleeing from place to place, or being slandered. In the eyes of the Father, I am worth much.

The world could viciously turn on Christians at any moment. I won't be afraid, because the Father is on my side watching out for my welfare.

Acknowledging the king

In 2017, the Chinese government began a new wave of restrictions on all registered religions, including Christianity.[5] The government's goal was to increase the Communist Party's control over religion. Underground Christians became more vulnerable to persecution, as well.

---

[5]"China tightens restrictions on religious freedom," *Yahoo*, September 8, 2017. https://www.yahoo.com/news/china-tightens-restrictions-religious-freedom-104907240.html (Current March 1, 2019).

Matthew 10:32–33 (CSB)

---

32 Therefore, everyone who will acknowledge me before others, I will also acknowledge him before my Father in heaven. 33 But whoever denies me before others, I will also deny him before my Father in heaven.

The fact I belong to Jesus and my testimony of what he has done for me are how I combat accusations of my enemies.

[The Christians] conquered [Satan]
by the blood of the Lamb
and by the word of their testimony;
for they did not love their lives
to the point of death.

Revelation 12:11 (CSB)

Even though the risk of legal action against Christians seems small in America, it sometimes happens. If I am arrested or sued in court, am I ready to acknowledge I am a follower of Jesus?

Most American Christians do not face persecution from the government, but many face hostile relatives, friends, and acquaintances. Will I acknowledge Jesus before them or will I disown him?

I am determined to always identify with Jesus. I will not be afraid, because Jesus will acknowledge me to the Father.

Do not fear

Even though opposition to the Kingdom message is likely, Jesus encouraged the disciples not to fear. I will ponder his reasons. When a crisis arises, will I be steadfast?

Nothing will be concealed. Living the Kingdom lifestyle and proclaiming the Kingdom message are not done in secret. Everything will be revealed eventually anyway, so I will boldly speak what Jesus said, and not be afraid.

They cannot kill the soul. Having the assurance of eternal life means threats of death are not important. Obeying the eternal judge is what is important, so I will not be afraid.

You are worth more than sparrows. God is interested in the small details of my life. Therefore, he is even more concerned for the big things. He thinks I'm important, so I will not be afraid.

Acknowledging the king. I will always acknowledge that I am a follower of Jesus. He will acknowledge me to the Father. I will not be afraid.

Do not fear. Even though dying as a martyr is possible, I will not be afraid. The truth will come out. Killing my body will not affect my eternal destiny. The Father knows all about my life. Jesus will acknowledge me to the Father. Therefore, I will not be afraid.

11

Loyalty to the king

Every man is called separately, and must follow alone...
[It is] Christ himself who compels him thus to break with his past.
Dietrich Bonhoeffer[1]

Even though my ancestors were church members, I had to decide for myself whether I would follow Jesus. I couldn't inherit faith from them. Family loyalty would not guarantee entrance into the Kingdom of Heaven, nor could it prevent me from entering. Loyalty to Jesus is more important than family loyalty. New life in Christ was a break with my selfish past. Now I am loyal to him. This chapter's passage discusses aspects of loyalty to Jesus.

Enemies in the family

At a family reunion, we had a Sunday worship service just for the family. There were about forty attending. The husband of my cousin is a pastor, so he was invited to give a short sermon. He preached a simple salvation message, "You must be born again." The wife of another cousin was offended by the gospel and that branch of the extended family boycotted family reunions from then on. Jesus acknowledged the Kingdom message is divisive, pitting even family members against each other.

Matthew 10:34–36 (CSB)[2]

---

34 Don't assume that I came to bring peace on the earth. I did not come to bring peace, but a sword. 35 For I came to turn

a man against his father,
a daughter against her mother,

---

[1]Bonhoeffer, pp. 105, 106.
[2]Luke 12:51–53 is a parallel passage.

a daughter-in-law against her mother-in-law;
36 and a man's enemies will be
the members of his household.

Family members who reject the Kingdom are often uncomfortable around those who embrace it.

I have become a stranger to my brothers
and a foreigner to my mother's sons
because zeal for your house has consumed me,
and the insults of those who insult you
have fallen on me.

Psalm 69:8–9 (CSB)

The person of Jesus and his Kingdom message is a challenge to every person. The message is more powerful than family loyalty. Some people think family loyalty is the most important allegiance one can have. However, for the disciple, loyalty to Jesus trumps family.

Who is unworthy?

I have a to-do list. There are so many things I need to do around here. Which one should I do first? I know. I'll prioritize my list and then do the most important one first. Then I'll make some progress. Jesus promised life for those who make him the top priority.

Matthew 10:37–39 (CSB)

---

37 The one who loves a father or mother more than me is not worthy of me; the one who loves a son or daughter more than me is not worthy of me. 38 And whoever doesn't take up his cross and follow me is not worthy of me. 39 Anyone who finds his life will lose it, and anyone who loses his life because of me will find it.

My love for Jesus must be greater than my love for my closest family member—father, mother, or child. When loyalty to family is more important than loyalty to Jesus, one is unworthy of a relationship with him.

Some family members may think they should be the most important thing in my life. They may be offended when they see that obeying Jesus comes first. Does loving Jesus as my first priority mean I love my family less?

This hope will not disappoint us, because God's love has been poured out in our hearts through the Holy Spirit who was given to us.

Romans 5:5 (CSB)

There is a big pitcher of ice tea in my refrigerator. When I pour the tea into my glass, it fills up. If I'm not paying attention, the glass may overflow, getting everything wet. God's love is supposed to fill my heart and splash on those around me. There is plenty for free refills.

However, the more I love Jesus, the more I am able to love my family. The capacity to love in the Kingdom is not a fixed quantity to be rationed to those around me. Love for the Lord gives me a supply of love that keeps splashing on those around me, even grumpy family members.

I follow Jesus, because I love him. However, it also costs condemnation by the world.

> Then Jesus said to his disciples, "If anyone wants to follow after me, let him deny himself, take up his cross, and follow me. For whoever wants to save his life will lose it, but whoever loses his life because of me will find it."
>
> Matthew 16:24–25 (CSB)

I studied logic in math class. When *A* is a statement, it is obvious that if *A* is true, then *not A* can't be true. If both seem true then there is a logical contradiction and I made a mistake in my math problem.

The Kingdom of Heaven seems to be upside down from my math class. Losing my life to find my life sounds like a contradiction. Jesus didn't make a mistake. Life in this world is not worth keeping when offered eternal life.

In New Testament times, crucifixion was a common punishment by the Romans.[3] For example, the two crucified with Jesus were criminals. People of that time were familiar with such scenes. Jesus faced condemnation very early in his ministry, so he knew the cross was waiting for him. He also knew the disciples would face the same. Tradition says all of the Twelve but John died as martyrs.[4] Throughout the centuries and even today, Christians have been killed for the faith.

Sometimes the world's condemnation is "in your face." At other times it is a "stab in the back" or a "thousand small cuts." Being unwilling to accept the world's condemnation for following Jesus makes one unworthy of a relationship with him.

> [Jesus said:] Those of you who do not give up everything you have cannot be my disciples.
>
> Luke 14:33 (NIV)

When I was about to find my first professional job, I came across Luke 14:33. I knew I was Jesus' disciple, but what did it mean for me to *give up* and what did *everything* include? After some prayerful meditation, I realized I had to give up my professional ambitions and also give up ambitions for some hobby projects. That was the application for me at that time. So instead of planning

---

[3]Bible commentators have a variety of interpretations for *take up his cross* in 10:38.
[4]Judas Iscariot who betrayed Jesus was replaced by Matthias who also died as a martyr.

my professional path myself, I relied on guidance by the Holy Spirit step by step. I lost my goals, but gained a professional life.

Martyrdom for Jesus' sake is a minor inconvenience compared to eternal life in the heavenly Kingdom. Being killed for Jesus' sake is the ultimate way to lose one's life. For those of us who rarely face the threat of death, "losing my life" can have other applications, such as giving up professional ambitions or giving up the American-Dream lifestyle to follow Jesus.

Who is rewarded?

My wife and I visited American friends in Malaysia. We had the opportunity to share Kingdom principles while there. Several local families showed us generous hospitality. God will reward them. We have embraced their examples.

Matthew 10:40–42 (CSB)

---

40 The one who welcomes you welcomes me, and the one who welcomes me welcomes him who sent me. 41 Anyone who welcomes a prophet because he is a prophet will receive a prophet's reward. And anyone who welcomes a righteous person because he's righteous will receive a righteous person's reward. 42 And whoever gives even a cup of cold water to one of these little ones because he is a disciple, truly I tell you, he will never lose his reward.

Even though the apostles faced persecution and rejection of the Kingdom message, there were some who received them and their message. There were some who gave them a place to stay as well.

Don't neglect to show hospitality, for by doing this some have welcomed angels as guests without knowing it.

Hebrews 13:2 (CSB)

The Old Testament has examples of hospitality to prophets. A widow in Zarephath hosted Elijah and was rewarded with food throughout a famine.[5] A woman in Shunem showed hospitality to Elisha and was rewarded when he raised her son from the dead.[6] Jesus' promise applies to those today who show hospitality to God's spokesmen.

While helping an international missions agency with their computers, I stayed at their guest house. I was joined at breakfast by a leader of churches in India and his wife and a leader of churches in Kenya. As we talked, I realized I was having breakfast with giants in the faith who were not famous. Jesus will reward our hosts for their gracious service.

Jesus promised even minimal hospitality, a cup of cold water, will be rewarded.

---

[5] 1 Kings 17:8–16.
[6] 2 Kings 4:8–37.

> A generous person will be enriched,
> and the one who gives a drink of water
> will receive water.

Proverbs 11:25 (CSB)

On a hot summer day, a handyman came to the house to fix a problem. My wife gave him a bottle of cold water. He thanked her and finished the project. We found out later he was saving money for a mission trip to China.

Jesus' promise is not limited to those who received the disciples as they traveled around Galilee. It applies to all who receive the Kingdom messengers, even when the Kingdom messenger is just an ordinary believer today. Even kindness to a "little one" is important. Receiving the Kingdom messenger is equivalent to receiving Jesus himself, and God will reward that hospitality.

Loyalty to the king

Jesus calls every disciple to live a life of complete loyalty to him. There may be distractions by family and persecution, but loyalty to him means I will treat other disciples as I would treat Jesus himself.

Enemies in the family. I am loyal to my relatives just because they are family, but loyalty to Jesus is even more important. I won't be surprised if a family member rejects the gospel and treats me as an enemy.

Who is unworthy? My life must be worthy of a relationship with Jesus, so I will not put a close family member ahead of him. I am willing to accept the world's condemnation, even if it means being a martyr. I'm willing to sacrifice the conveniences of life to follow Jesus.

Who is rewarded? Hospitality toward Kingdom messengers is like receiving Jesus himself. Even simple kindnesses to ordinary believers will be rewarded in the Kingdom of Heaven.

Loyalty to the king. Will I be loyal to King Jesus? Is he more important than my family? Is he more important than my plans and ambitions or life itself? Will I welcome ordinary humble believers just as I would receive the king? Yes, I will be loyal to the king.

12

Apostles of the Kingdom

When Christ calls a man, he bids him come and die.

Dietrich Bonhoeffer[1]

Bonhoeffer had no reservations about following the call of Jesus. Selfishness had to die. Because Jesus went willingly to the cross, Bonhoeffer knew discipleship might entail the same. After being imprisoned by the Nazis for about two years, he was executed.

Commission. Jesus gave instructions to the Twelve for a specific mission. After the resurrection, he commissioned his followers to spread the gospel throughout the world. I will apply his instructions to my life whether close to home or traveling half way around the world.

Expect opposition. Jesus warned the apostles to expect opposition. I must be innocent of the evil around me, but not gullible. I will be prudent in the face of opposition, but will stand firm when arrested, betrayed, hated, and slandered.

Do not fear. Jesus admonished the apostles not to be afraid, even when threatened with death. The heavenly Father cares for me, and Jesus will acknowledge me to the Father, so I won't be afraid of opposition.

Loyalty to the king. Jesus calls a disciple to complete loyalty. He is more important than family, daily concerns, and life itself. My loyalty will be expressed in hospitality and kindness to ordinary humble believers, because they represent the king.

---

[1]Bonhoeffer, p. 99.

Apostles of the Kingdom. Jesus' instructions to the Twelve about their mission are applicable to me. Will I respond with obedience and steadfastness? The mission means proclaiming the Kingdom is near and validating the message with healings, resurrections, cleansings, and deliverances. But there will be opposition and persecution. I will not be afraid, but will remain loyal to my king.

Part III

The Kingdom is like ...

13

Why parables?

You can only learn what obedience is by obeying. It is no use asking questions; for it is only through obedience that you come to learn the truth.

Dietrich Bonhoeffer[1]

Some things must be learned by experience. Reading a manual does not adequately teach me how to fasten a bolt with a wrench. Feeling the wrench in my hand is necessary. The Kingdom of Heaven must be learned through experience. The parables make sense to the obedient ones, living the Kingdom lifestyle. To learn the truth about the Kingdom, I must obey Jesus' teaching.

This discourse consists of a series of parables. Jesus told some parables to the crowds. Jesus knew few could hear him when he sat on the shore, so he sat in a boat a bit out from shore where his voice would carry. Jesus told other parables just to the disciples. He also explained some of them to the disciples privately.

Scholars have studied these and other parables in depth, so there are many approaches.[2] Here, a devotional approach is taken, applying the basic message of each parable. Understanding the Kingdom of Heaven is my goal. This chapter skips ahead to Jesus' explanation about parables, rather than proceeding from beginning to end. Later chapters consider the parables themselves.

Matthew 13:1–3,10–17,34–35 (CSB)[3]

---

1 On that day Jesus went out of the house and was sitting by the sea. 2 Such large crowds gathered around him that he got into a boat and sat down, while the whole crowd stood on the shore.

3 Then he told them many things in parables, saying: . . .

10 Then the disciples came up and asked him, "Why are you speaking to them in parables?"

---

[1]Bonhoeffer, p. 86.
[2]Carson, pp. 301–304.
[3]Mark 4:11–12 and Luke 10:23–24 are parallels to parts of this passage.

11 He answered, "Because the secrets of the kingdom of heaven have been given for you to know, but it has not been given to them. 12 For whoever has, more will be given to him, and he will have more than enough; but whoever does not have, even what he has will be taken away from him. 13 That is why I speak to them in parables, because looking they do not see, and hearing they do not listen or understand. 14 Isaiah's prophecy is fulfilled in them, which says:

> You will listen and listen,
> but never understand;
> you will look and look,
> but never perceive.
> 15 For this people's heart has grown callous;
> their ears are hard of hearing,
> and they have shut their eyes;
> otherwise they might see with their eyes,
> and hear with their ears, and
> understand with their hearts,
> and turn back—
> and I would heal them.

16 "Blessed are your eyes because they do see, and your ears because they do hear. 17 For truly I tell you, many prophets and righteous people longed to see the things you see but didn't see them, to hear the things you hear but didn't hear them..."

34 Jesus told the crowds all these things in parables, and he did not tell them anything without a parable, 35 so that what was spoken through the prophet might be fulfilled:

> I will open my mouth in parables;
> I will declare things kept secret
> from the foundation of the world.

Jesus explained to the disciples why he used parable so much.[4] His goal was to teach his disciples about the Kingdom of Heaven. Parables were an effective teaching method. He knew the crowds, and especially the religious leaders, would not understand, because their hearts were resistant.

Paul saw the same resistance.

For it is written:

> I will destroy the wisdom of the wise,
> and I will set aside the intelligence of the intelligent.

---

[4]In verses 14 and 15, Jesus quoted Isaiah 6:9–10. In verse 35, Matthew quoted Psalm 78:2.

> Where is the one who is wise? Where is the teacher of the law?
> Where is the debater of this age? Hasn't God made the world's
> wisdom foolish? For since, in God's wisdom, the world did not
> know God through wisdom, God was pleased to save those who
> believe through the foolishness of what is preached.
>
> 1 Corinthians 1:19–21 (CSB)

A *wise* man in these verses is like a modern expert. An *intelligent* person is like an intellectual. A *teacher of the law* is like a theologian. A *debater* is like a lawyer.

In the 1980s, church-growth seminars were popular. Experts from advertising, public relations, and group dynamics were supposed to show your pastor how to make your church into a megachurch. The ideas were okay on a human level, but weren't very effective for churches. The experts did not understand the parables about the Kingdom of Heaven.

Intellectuals like to espouse new ideas that make God unnecessary. In the 1960s and 1970s, gurus from India came to Western countries and each developed a following. Celebrities endorsed so-and-so. *New Age* became a label for a collection of mystical ideas and superstitions. Intellectuals defended rejection of the God of the Bible with convoluted arguments, none of which were based on Kingdom principles.

Fads in theology come along from time to time, doubting the truth of the Bible. In the early twentieth century, there was form criticism. In the 1960s, there was situation ethics and liberation theology. The Kingdom of Heaven was once a favorite, too. Even if embraced by popular culture, fads in theology have never affected the real Kingdom of Heaven.

Modern lawyers push for "separation of church and state," which they claim means atheism should be the religion enforced by the government. Pages and pages of legal briefs present their positions. Hours and hours of court arguments try to convince the highest courts. God knows atheism is foolishness.[5] All their legal briefs and court arguments don't convince him, and he is the judge of the highest court.

Forgiveness of my sins through the death of Jesus on the cross, and his triumphant resurrection are dismissed by experts, intellectuals, liberal theologians, and worldly lawyers, but God's wisdom is deeper than human wisdom. God's ways are truth and righteousness. Compared to God's eternal wisdom, human wisdom is foolishness. God's wisdom about the Kingdom of Heaven is revealed in the parables of Jesus.

> For the word of the cross is foolishness to those who are perishing,
> but it is the power of God to us who are being saved.
>
> 1 Corinthians 1:18 (CSB)

While my friends were having an animated conversation, I had no idea what they were talking about. Eventually, I realized they were talking about

---

[5]Psalm 14:1.

a new movie. I didn't understand the conversation, because I hadn't seen the movie.

Jesus explained why he used parables. The secrets of the Kingdom are revealed to the citizens of the Kingdom. When a person lives the Kingdom lifestyle, God reveals many things. Faith is a prerequisite. When one lives in the Kingdom, Jesus' parables make sense, and through them, one learns even more about Kingdom living.

Atheists have a hard time understanding the Kingdom. They misinterpret Christians' motives. They twist Scripture passages and misapply Christian doctrine. Some people claim to be Christians, sit in church sometimes, but live and think like atheists. Jesus explained they have calloused hearts, hearts without faith. That is why their eyes can be open, but they cannot perceive. They can pass a hearing test, but cannot comprehend.

When a person hears the call of Christ to believe and to become a disciple, he can understand a little of the Kingdom message. If he says "Yes!" then his understanding of the Kingdom will grow because of his faith. However, if he rejects the Kingdom message, his unbelief will choke out the little he did understand, and he will be more ignorant of the Kingdom than before.

When one has faith, he has the context and experience to learn from the parables of Jesus. Understanding a parable means one draws relationships between elements of the story and things in life. Then one's understanding of life is richer. An unbeliever doesn't have the context, so there is no life to enrich.

14

Parables of the Kingdom

The call goes forth, and is at once followed by the response of obedience.
The response of the disciples is an act of obedience, not a confession of faith
in Jesus.

Dietrich Bonhoeffer[1]

Bonhoeffer applied the parable of the sower to discipleship. The sower spreads the call to discipleship. The good ground responds with obedience which results in an abundant harvest.

Reciting a list of doctrines, as in a traditional confession of faith, may be necessary to join an organization, but becoming a disciple of Jesus is different than knowing doctrine. Following Jesus means doing what he says.

This chapter considers the parables of the sower, the wheat and tares, the mustard seed, and the yeast.

A sower

Wheat grew in the field next to my grandfather's house. I knew each stalk had grown from one seed. When I took a close look at a stalk of ripe wheat, there were many wheat seeds on that one stalk. When the soil and weather are good, a small investment in seeds produces a big return.

Matthew 13:3–9,18–23 (CSB)[2]

---

3 Consider the sower who went out to sow. 4 As he sowed, some seed fell along the path, and the birds came and devoured them. 5 Other seed fell on rocky ground where it didn't have much soil, and it grew up quickly since the soil wasn't deep. 6 But when the

---

[1] Bonhoeffer, p. 61.
[2] Mark 4:3–9,13–20 and Luke 8:5–8,11–15 are parallel passages.

sun came up, it was scorched, and since it had no root, it withered away. 7 Other seed fell among thorns, and the thorns came up and choked it. 8 Still other seed fell on good ground and produced fruit: some a hundred, some sixty, and some thirty times what was sown. 9 Let anyone who has ears listen...

18 So listen to the parable of the sower: 19 When anyone hears the word about the kingdom and doesn't understand it, the evil one comes and snatches away what was sown in his heart. This is the one sown along the path. 20 And the one sown on rocky ground— this is one who hears the word and immediately receives it with joy. 21 But he has no root and is short-lived. When distress or persecution comes because of the word, immediately he falls away. 22 Now the one sown among the thorns—this is one who hears the word, but the worries of this age and the deceitfulness of wealth choke the word, and it becomes unfruitful. 23 But the one sown on the good ground—this is one who hears and understands the word, who does produce fruit and yields: some a hundred, some sixty, some thirty times what was sown.

This story is traditionally called the *parable of the sower*, even though the sower is mentioned only briefly. Jesus told the parable to the crowd, but explained it to the disciples in private.

Hard ground. Jesus explained the *seed* is the Kingdom message. When someone rejects the Kingdom message, their thinking becomes foolish and worthless.

> For though [the pagans] knew God, they did not glorify him as God or show gratitude. Instead, their thinking became worthless, and their senseless hearts were darkened. Claiming to be wise, they became fools.
>
> Romans 1:21–22 (CSB)

I can imagine situations such as the following where someone has a hard heart and the devil steals the word away.

The pastor was preaching his heart out. Little Johnny was old enough to understand, but was playing a video game. (At least he was quiet!) Mom was wondering whether the preacher would go so long the roast would burn. Dad was eager to get to the golf course for his one-o'clock tee time.

In the church youth group, the youth pastor was preaching a rousing message while Jimmy was trying to get up the nerve to ask the cute girl across the room for a date.

On the street, Joe was talking about Jesus with a guy who was wondering where he was going to get his next hit.

The natural world is the first evidence of God's grace one encounters, but the pagans chose idolatry instead. Today, we have the testimony of the apostles that Jesus rose from the dead, but people choose selfish convenience and entertainment instead. The Kingdom message can be presented in many ways, but the devil uses many distractions to steal the word.

Rocky soil. Hearts like hard ground resist the gospel. Hearts like rocky soil don't endure testing of faith.

> Blessed is the one who endures trials, because when he has stood the test he will receive the crown of life that God has promised to those who love him.
>
> James 1:12 (CSB)

When I was in high school, my church youth group went on a camping trip. We stayed in flimsy cabins out in the woods. While we were there, a hurricane came through the area. We quickly left the camp site to stay in nearby university dorms. During the night we had a prayer meeting and many in the group committed their lives to the Lord. When we got back home, some continued to grow in their Christian walk, but some reverted to their old worldly ways as soon as they returned to their old friends. They did not want to be ridiculed for the faith. They were like rocky soil where the Kingdom message wilted when persecution came.

When one becomes a believer, life changes. There is the initial elation of receiving forgiveness, but new experiences test one's faith. When the commitment is deep, the believer passes the test and God rewards him. If the commitment to Jesus is superficial, he falls back into the old lifestyle.

Thorns in soil. Hearts like soil with weeds are distracted by the world's attractions.

> But encourage each other daily, while it is still called today, so that none of you is hardened by sin's deception.
>
> Hebrews 3:13 (CSB)

Many teenagers participate in a church youth group, and then they go to college. On the first Sunday of the semester, many college students were in church. When Mom called, they could say, "Yes, I've been to church." The rest of the semester they didn't show up. I suppose partying Saturday night and sleeping in on Sunday morning were more important.

Distractions from Kingdom living can be subtle. Some people chase after success and the American Dream. They spend every weekend having fun, for example, snowmobiling in the woods of Wisconsin, splashing in the surf in Florida, hiking in the mountains, canoeing on the lake, and a thousand other pastimes. They might be in church on Christmas, Easter, and Mother's Day.

I need the encouragement of other believers who help me stay focused on Kingdom living. Misplaced priorities is a symptom of sin's deception. A life full of distractions is like the soil overgrown with thorns, choking out the fruitfulness of the Kingdom message.

Good soil. Hearts like hard ground, rocky soil, and soil with weeds don't produce good fruit, but hearts open to the Holy Spirit produce abundant spiritual fruit.

> But the fruit of the Spirit is love, joy, peace, patience, kindness, goodness, faithfulness, gentleness, and self-control. The law is not against such things.
>
> Galatians 5:22–23 (CSB)

My neighbor planted a peach tree. After a few years, even though it was still a sapling, it flowered and produced delicious peaches.

When a person is receptive to the Kingdom message and lets it take root in his life, it produces good fruit. Paul wrote to the Galatians about "fruit of the Spirit." From the beginning, those were the qualities I wanted in my life. A small investment of the Word of God in a receptive heart produces an abundant life.

Wheat and tares

In kindergarten, we learn we are supposed to "play nice." In other words, don't hurt the other kids. As we get older we learn we should not "lie, cheat, or steal," and certainly never murder. Sometimes we see acts of kindness and courtesy, but it is also obvious some people do not "play nice."

Matthew 13:24–30,36–43 (CSB)

24 [Jesus] presented another parable to them: "The kingdom of heaven may be compared to a man who sowed good seed in his field. 25 But while people were sleeping, his enemy came, sowed weeds among the wheat, and left. 26 When the plants sprouted and produced grain, then the weeds also appeared. 27 The landowner's servants came to him and said, 'Master, didn't you sow good seed in your field? Then where did the weeds come from?'

28 " 'An enemy did this,' he told them.

" 'So, do you want us to go and pull them up?' the servants asked him.

29 " 'No,' he said. 'When you pull up the weeds, you might also uproot the wheat with them. 30 Let both grow together until the harvest. At harvest time I'll tell the reapers: Gather the weeds first and tie them in bundles to burn them, but collect the wheat in my barn.' " ...

36 Then [Jesus] left the crowds and went into the house. His disciples approached him and said, "Explain to us the parable of the weeds in the field."

37 He replied: "The one who sows the good seed is the Son of Man; 38 the field is the world; and the good seed—these are the children of the kingdom. The weeds are the children of the evil one, 39 and the enemy who sowed them is the devil. The harvest is the end of the age, and the harvesters are angels. 40 Therefore, just as the weeds are gathered and burned in the fire, so it will be at the end of the age. 41 The Son of Man will send out his angels, and they will gather from his kingdom all who cause sin and those guilty of lawlessness. 42 They will throw them into the blazing furnace where there will be weeping and gnashing of teeth. 43 Then the righteous will shine like the sun in their Father's kingdom. Let anyone who has ears listen."

Based on KJV wording, this parable is often called the *parable of the wheat and tares.* Like the parable of the sower, Jesus told this parable to the crowd, but interpreted it for the disciples in private. The parable illustrates the difference between the world and the disciples.

[Jesus said:] I am not praying that you [heavenly Father] take [my disciples] out of the world but that you protect them from the evil one. They are not of the world, just as I am not of the world. Sanctify them by the truth; your word is truth.

John 17:15–17 (CSB)

In its early days, the Internet was a place where everyone "played nice." Scientists exchanged data and email over long distances in just a moment. One's emails were all from acquaintances. Discussions were courteous and helpful, even when people disagreed. As the Internet became a valuable business tool, greed and hatred entered the Internet world, so now there are stolen credit cards numbers, misinformation, deceptive advertising, identity theft, email spam, phishing for personal information, and hacking for industrial secrets. No longer does everyone "play nice." The good and bad operate side by side.

Whenever I read about evil oppression, exploitation, murder, and destruction, I wonder, "Why doesn't God just get rid of that guy?" This parable explains Jesus will do so at the end of the age when he rules over the whole world, but for now, he is letting the children of the devil live side by side with the children of the Kingdom, while the Kingdom matures.

A mustard seed and yeast

A few people agreed to start a home Bible study at Barbara's house. Over time, the numbers grew and the people matured. Even without recruiters, the Lord sent those who needed to be there. In the Kingdom, small beginnings grow into large mature results like a mustard seed grows into a large shrub.

Matthew 13:31–33 (CSB)[3]

---

31 [Jesus] presented another parable to them: "The kingdom of heaven is like a mustard seed that a man took and sowed in his field. 32 It's the smallest of all the seeds, but when grown, it's taller than the garden plants and becomes a tree, so that the birds of the sky come and nest in its branches."

33 He told them another parable: "The kingdom of heaven is like leaven that a woman took and mixed into fifty pounds of flour until all of it was leavened."

A mustard seed. Mustard seeds are the smallest one might see in a vegetable garden. The plant grows into a sizable shrub. All of Jesus' audience were familiar with mustard plants.

Do not despise this small beginning.
Zechariah 4:10 (TLB)

After the Babylonian captivity, Zerubbabel began to rebuild the temple, but it was modest compared to Solomon's temple. Zechariah told him not to be discouraged by the small beginning, because God was supporting him.

The Kingdom was very small during the ministry of Jesus. Peter, Andrew, James, and John were not important people. The twelve disciples whom Jesus sent out were not an army. After Jesus' ascension, the 120 in the upper room were not a movement. A few decades later, when Paul and Silas came to Thessalonica, their accusers referred to them as "These that have turned the world upside down."[4] Today, even though there is still great opposition and persecution, millions around the world receive the Kingdom gladly.

Yeast. Abraham's wife Sarah prepared for a banquet the same amount of flour mentioned in verse 33.[5] In this parable, the amount of flour probably represents the largest batch a woman would prepare at one time.[6] One can apply the flour of this parable to the life of a Christian. The gospel had saturated Paul's life, but he was still pressing for more.

Brothers and sisters, I do not consider myself to have taken hold of [the goal]. But one thing I do: Forgetting what is behind and

---

[3]Mark 4:30–32 and Luke 13:18–21 are parallel passages.
[4]Acts 17:6 (KJV).
[5]Genesis 18:6.
[6]The CSB's *fifty pounds* translates the Greek "three *satas*," a measure of volume. No one is sure how much a *sata* was, but some estimate one *sata* to be more than five gallons which means three *satas* of flour might weigh fifty pounds (Carson, p. 319).

> reaching forward to what is ahead, I pursue as my goal the prize promised by God's heavenly call in Christ Jesus.
>
> Philippians 3:13–14 (CSB)

I became a born-again believer when I was ten years old. Through my teens I read the Bible often, and the church I attended taught the Bible. In high school, I began to evaluate what I read in school according to what the Bible says. Much of our reading assumed people are basically good which is not what the Bible teaches. In college, I had to learn to related to ungodly friends. When I began my career, I confronted business-ethics issues. Along the way, I learned to love other Christians from many denominations and streams. God used the Kingdom message to transform my character bit by bit. Of course, I made plenty of mistakes, but God was faithful.

In the beginning, yeast is small, like a mustard seed, but a little bit of yeast grows and spreads throughout a lump of dough. The action of the yeast reminds me that the Kingdom message will permeate my life gradually if I will receive it.

Parables of the Kingdom

Jesus used many common features of life in first-century Galilee to illustrate his teaching. All the farmers were familiar with wheat, soils, and weeds. All the women were familiar with mustard, flour, and yeast. I may not live in a village in Galilee, but studying the history and culture of ancient times has helped me understand Jesus' parables.

Even though I'm not a farmer, I recognize how people respond to the gospel in different ways. My city may not have wheat fields, but I can see how believers and worldly people live side by side. I don't have a garden with mustard plants, but I know small seeds can produce big shrubs. I don't know how to make bread from scratch, but the smell of fresh baked bread tells me the tiny yeast has done its job. The parables reveal the Kingdom of Heaven.

15

More parables of the Kingdom

> *Cheap grace means grace as a doctrine, a principle, a system. It means forgiveness of sins proclaimed as a general truth, the love of God taught as the Christian "conception" of God...*
>
> *Cheap grace means the justification of sin without the justification of the sinner...*
>
> *Cheap grace is the preaching of forgiveness without requiring repentance, baptism without church discipline, Communion without confession, absolution without personal confession. Cheap grace is grace without discipleship, grace without the cross, grace without Jesus Christ, living and incarnate...*
>
> *[Costly] grace is costly because it calls us to follow, and it is grace because it calls us to follow Jesus Christ... Above all, it is costly because it cost God the life of his Son.*
>
> Dietrich Bonhoeffer[1]

Bonhoeffer compared the parable of the treasure in the field to God's costly grace. Doctrines and systematic theologies don't reveal the Kingdom of Heaven. When one obeys the call to follow Jesus, one experiences God's costly grace and all the Kingdom means. Then the parables begin to make sense.

This chapter considers the parables of the treasure, the pearl, and a net.

Treasure and a pearl

At an antique auction, I bought a dining room table and six chairs with a black walnut finish. Later, when we refinished them, the old finish was stripped

---

[1] Bonhoeffer, pp. 45–48.

away, revealing a dramatic curly oak grain. The beauty of the grain was initially hidden.

Matthew 13:44–46 (CSB)

---

44 The kingdom of heaven is like treasure, buried in a field, that a man found and reburied. Then in his joy he goes and sells everything he has and buys that field.

45 Again, the kingdom of heaven is like a merchant in search of fine pearls. 46 When he found one priceless pearl, he went and sold everything he had and bought it.

This passage is a pair of parables. The treasure and the pearl are both extremely valuable.

Treasure. The Kingdom of Heaven is like a treasure.

For the word of the cross is foolishness to those who are perishing, but it is the power of God to us who are being saved...
But as it is written:

What no eye has seen, no ear has heard,
and no human heart has conceived—
God has prepared these things for those who love him.

Now God has revealed these things to us by the Spirit, since the Spirit searches everything, even the depths of God.
1 Corinthians 1:18; 2:9–10 (CSB)

In the parable of the treasure, the value of the field was hidden and was not obvious to everyone. Similarly, the value of the Kingdom is not apparent to unbelievers.[2] The message of the cross is the gate to the Kingdom, but it is foolishness to the worldly mind, so its value is hidden.

How valuable is the Kingdom? So valuable that a man would sell all he has to raise enough money to buy the field and the treasure in it. Extreme action is necessary for an extreme treasure. God has prepared for us a life that is unimaginably wonderful.

A pearl. The Kingdom of Heaven is like the expensive pearl. Its benefits are more valuable than anything else.

For the kingdom of God is not eating and drinking, but righteousness, peace, and joy in the Holy Spirit.
Romans 14:17 (CSB)

---

[2] 1 Corinthians 2:14.

Righteousness, peace and joy are personal benefits of the Kingdom to me. When I was ten years old, I thought being a good boy would get me into heaven. Then I found out being good was not enough, so I asked God to forgive me of my sins and come into my life. That is when I experienced the gift of righteousness. Since then, my behavior and thoughts have improved bit by bit. Righteousness is a benefit of the Kingdom.

I have learned to trust God with my career. Knowing I am loved by God no matter what happens at my job has given me peace in my career. Peace is a benefit of the Kingdom.

Because I know I am God's child, I can smile most of the time. A smile comes from deep inside, not from fun or pleasant circumstances. I smile at strangers on the street. I can smile when someone is cranky or rude. I can brush off disappointments, because I know my Father in heaven has something better planned for me. Joy is a benefit of the Kingdom.

A net

My father had a cast net. It was round with weights on the edge. When thrown off the end of a dock, it spread out into a big circle. With the rope tied to his wrist, he drew his catch up onto the dock. He kept those small enough for bait and threw the rest back into the water.

Matthew 13:47–50 (CSB)

---

47 Again, the kingdom of heaven is like a large net thrown into the sea. It collected every kind of fish, 48 and when it was full, they dragged it ashore, sat down, and gathered the good fish into containers, but threw out the worthless ones. 49 So it will be at the end of the age. The angels will go out, separate the evil people from the righteous, 50 and throw them into the blazing furnace, where there will be weeping and gnashing of teeth.

This parable presents a picture of fishermen sorting their catch, keeping the edible fish and throwing away the worthless ones. The interpretation of this parable is similar to the parable of the wheat and tares, describing what will happen when Jesus returns.[3]

The kingdom of the world has become the kingdom
of our Lord and of his Christ,
and he will reign forever and ever.

Revelation 11:15 (CSB)

Several of Jesus' disciples were fishermen, so his parable described a familiar scene, fishermen sorting their catch. Jesus clearly interpreted the parable.

---

[3]13:36–43.

At the end of the age, the wicked will be separated from the citizens of the Kingdom by God's angels. His Kingdom will be cleansed of those who do injustice.

Jesus has received authority over this world, so today, people have a choice. Which side are you on? For the Messiah or against the Messiah?

More parables of the Kingdom

The disciples were familiar with the characters in Jesus' parables. They knew merchants in town. Some of them were fishermen. The parables in this chapter were familiar scenes.

Today, we see similar scenes. Sometimes an investor will buy property because he thinks oil is in the ground. An art dealer will bid for a painting at auction because he recognizes great art. A sport fisherman today will keep the big ones for dinner, but will throw back the inedible ones. The parables reveal the Kingdom of Heaven.

16

The Kingdom is like ...

Happy are they who, knowing that [costly] grace, can live in the world without being of it, who, by following Jesus Christ, are so assured of their heavenly citizenship that they are truly free to live their lives in this world.
Dietrich Bonhoeffer[1]

Citizens of a country understand its history and culture. They may visit another country, but they are always aware of their privileges and responsibilities toward their home country. When one has experienced God's grace, understanding the Kingdom parables is easy. The world may seem like a foreign country, but applying the parables to life is obvious.

Treasures new and old

My neighbor decorated her house for every holiday. Her attic and garage must have been stuffed with curios, dishes, linens, and banners. Each one was associated with a memory of a special person or event. I'm sure she considered each one a treasure.

Matthew 13:51–52 (CSB)

[Jesus asked,] 51 "Have you understood all these things?"
[The disciples] answered him, "Yes."
52 "Therefore," he said to them, "every teacher of the law who has become a disciple in the kingdom of heaven is like the owner of a house who brings out of his storeroom treasures new and old."

In Jesus' time, a *scribe* (KJV) was a *teacher of the law* (CSB). Such a professional was knowledgeable about the Old Testament Scriptures. If a teacher of the law

[1] Bonhoeffer, p. 60.

received the Kingdom message, he would be able to share both new truths about the Kingdom and the old truths of the Old Testament Scriptures.

> All Scripture is inspired by God and is profitable for teaching, for rebuking, for correcting, for training in righteousness, so that the man of God may be complete, equipped for every good work.
>
> 2 Timothy 3:16–17 (CSB)

I attended a seminar where a Philosophy professor read a paper he had presented at a conference. He used big words and long sentences with complex grammar and very abstract ideas. If I concentrated, I might figure out what the words meant, but I had only a vague idea of what he was talking about. When the hour was over, I was exhausted.

Jesus did not teach like a Philosophy professor. Jesus told stories everyone in the crowd could understand. He would say, "The Kingdom of Heaven is like..." His parables revealed new truths which had been "hidden since the creation of the world."[2] Those who received the Kingdom message became disciples. They understood the parables, because they were experiencing Kingdom living, but the new Kingdom truths did not make the old Scriptures obsolete.

If I study the entire Bible, then I will have treasures to share with others, old and new. If I explain the Kingdom with stories instead of abstract academic jargon, then listeners will understand what I am saying and some may receive the Kingdom message.

The Kingdom is like ...

Jesus used parables to explain what the Kingdom of Heaven is like, why some people reject the gospel, how the Kingdom grows, how following Jesus is worth the sacrifice, and the fact this world will be cleansed of evil.

Why parables? When I read Jesus' parables, I make connections between the familiar features of the story and spiritual truths about the Kingdom of Heaven. Because I am a believer, I have experienced the Kingdom in some areas. This context helps me understand the parables.

A sower. The parable of the sower presents several kinds of soil. Jesus interpreted the parable for us. The seed is the gospel and the soils represent various kinds of people. The best result is when a person lets the Kingdom message produce abundant spiritual fruit.

---

[2]13:35 (NIV).

Wheat and tares. Jesus also interpreted the parable of the wheat and tares. The wheat represents disciples and the weeds represent unbelievers. The parable explains God's plan for letting the Kingdom mature on earth until the end of the age.

A mustard seed and yeast. Even though the Kingdom of Heaven began with a small group of disciples, it has grown to millions and millions of believers. From the beginning, God planned for it to grow, like a mustard seed grows into a large shrub. Similarly, yeast is tiny, almost invisible, but it grows and spreads throughout a lump of dough. The dough can represent large or small things. The Kingdom of Heaven will influence society when people will receive it, and the Kingdom message will transform my life as I apply the Scriptures.

Treasure and a pearl. How valuable is the Kingdom of Heaven? It is so valuable a man would exchange everything he has to get the treasure. The Kingdom life is more wonderful than anyone can imagine.

A net. Jesus has authority over this world. When he returns he will cleanse his Kingdom. The angels will separate believers from the wicked. People today have a choice: receive the Messiah or reject him.

Treasures new and old. The teachings of the Old Testament and New Testament are like old and new treasures. When I share the Kingdom message, I will follow Jesus' example, using the familiar for illustrations.

The Kingdom is like ... The Kingdom of Heaven is not a deep mystery only special people can understand. Jesus' audience included farmers, homemakers, merchants, and fishermen. Jesus taught using parables with familiar scenes from life to explain how people respond to the Kingdom message and how the Kingdom works. I can understand spiritual Kingdom principles, because I have tasted life in the Kingdom of Heaven.

Part IV

Greatest in the Kingdom

17

Who is the greatest?

This community of strangers possesses no inherent right of its own... they renounce every right of their own and live for the sake of Jesus Christ.
Dietrich Bonhoeffer[1]

Americans are very conscious of their rights. The US Constitution has ten amendments called the Bill of Rights. If someone around me feels his rights have been violated, I will certainly hear about it with loud complaints.

The disciples thought being an honored member of the Kingdom of Heaven ought to carry some special rights and privileges. Surely whoever is greatest in the Kingdom has some good perquisites and fringe benefits. But the disciples were wrong. The Kingdom of Heaven is not like America. The greatest disciple claims no rights of his own.

People have many strategies for becoming great in the Kingdom. Be at church whenever the doors are open and do all the activities. Get on the Board, chair an important committee, or hold a high office in the denomination. Become a well-known worship leader, a world-renowned motivational speaker, or a best-selling author. Heal many people or cast out many demons. There are many strategies for becoming famous and influential in church circles. Is that the same as "great in the Kingdom of Heaven"?

Like the disciples, I have often wondered what can I do to please the king and get promoted? The world's pattern is based on achievements. However, that is not the Kingdom of Heaven pattern. The disciples were probably motivated by selfish ambition. Maybe I have been, too.

Matthew 18:1–4 (CSB)[2]

---

1 At that time the disciples came to Jesus and asked, "So who is greatest in the kingdom of heaven?"

---

[1] Bonhoeffer, p. 122.
[2] Mark 9:33–37 and Luke 9:46–48 are parallel passages.

2 He called a child and had him stand among them. 3 "Truly I tell you," he said, "unless you turn and become like children, you will never enter the kingdom of heaven. 4 Therefore, whoever humbles himself like this child—this one is the greatest in the kingdom of heaven."

A word study on pride and humility using a concordance will yield a huge number of references. The whole Bible is full of teaching on humility. This chapter is just an introduction.

Child-like

While visiting a friend's house, we played guitars and sang some songs. A little one, perhaps three years old, was interested in my guitar. I let her strum while I held the frets and then she and I sang a song she knew.

> All of you clothe yourselves with humility toward one another, because
>
>> God resists the proud
>> but gives grace to the humble.
>
> 1 Peter 5:5 (CSB)

What characteristic of a small child is necessary to enter the Kingdom? Jesus focused on humility. A small child understands the difference between me and my friends and Mom, Dad, and their friends. Little ones are loved and protected by the big ones, but there is no doubt big ones are in charge. I have no doubt God is bigger than me. He loves me and protects me, and I know who is in charge.

Small children also have no sense of social status. They will play with anyone, the kid down the street, the new kid at church, and even Uncle Eddie, if he will get down on a child's level. Humility with others is being willing to socialize with anyone.

The disciples asked, "Who is the greatest?" The answer is "Whoever humbles himself." The greatest in the Kingdom is the humble believer whose only goal is to be a faithful servant to the king. The humble servant doesn't care about being greatest.

Humble

In high school, I was voted "most academic." I felt honored. When I got to college, I found there were many others who were more academic than I.

> Do not think of yourself more highly than you ought.
>
> Romans 12:3 (NIV)

Pride is a subtle thing. Someone might say, "I've been humble all my life, and I'm proud of it!" Pride has crept into my life through simple things like achieving a goal, making good grades in junior high school, or getting an article published in a magazine. Sometimes a friend will give me a sincere compliment. The temptation to be proud pops up. "I guess I really am great, if you say so!"

Each time the temptation pops up, I must remind myself who made me, who provides for me, and who blesses me, namely, my heavenly Father. I can't take credit for what he does. By the way, I've had to learn to receive compliments graciously, too.

> Honor one another above yourselves.
>
> Romans 12:10 (NIV)

At a church dinner, who gets to go through the buffet line first? The honored guest, of course. What does the honored guest do? He insists someone else go first. He honors others above himself.

Low self-esteem can be oppressive and debilitating, but high self-esteem seems to be the same as pride. The source of good self-esteem is the fact God loves me, not my accomplishments and not what others think of me. Very high self-esteem is proper, because God loves me very much. On a social level, I must honor others. So, I have very high self-esteem, and I esteem you higher than myself.

Who is the greatest?

The disciples were probably jockeying for prestigious positions in the Kingdom. At supper before his crucifixion, Jesus took a towel and washed the disciples feet. This was typically the duty of the lowest slave. Through this act, Jesus illustrated the kind of humility a disciple should have.[3]

Jesus called a child and presented him as an example of who could be greatest.[4] The believer who is humble like a small child is the one Jesus regards as great. That believer is focused on being a faithful servant to the king. The status symbols of greatness are irrelevant.

Pride is the opposite of humility. Pride easily creeps into my attitude, but I must remember the heavenly Father blesses me with all I need. I must not presume to take credit for what he does. The humble disciple does not denigrate himself. God loves him. Humility is honoring others more than myself, because God loves them, too. The greatest in the Kingdom of Heaven is the disciple who is humble like a child, who rejects a prideful attitude, and who honors others more than himself.

---

[3]John 13:3–15.
[4]18:1–4.

18

Protect a child

In Jesus [the disciples] have apprehended the loving-kindness of the Father.
In the name of the Son of God they are privileged to call God Father.

Dietrich Bonhoeffer[1]

As a child, I felt the loving concern of my father for my welfare. As a young adult away from home, I felt the same concern from older men in my church. They were father-figures to me. Their examples helped me understand the love the heavenly Father has for me.

The humble disciple is greatest in the Kingdom of Heaven, because the heavenly Father loves him. A humble disciple is like a child whom Jesus welcomes, protects, and seeks. The little ones are precious to the heavenly Father.

Welcome

I was early for church. When I came into the sanctuary, the only person there was a visitor seated on the back row. So, I greeted him, sat down, and started a conversation. As the service was about to start, he told me his name and I realized he was the guest preacher that day.

Matthew 18:5 (CSB)[2]

---

5 And whoever welcomes one child like this in my name welcomes me.

The humble disciple is precious to the heavenly Father. Jesus identifies with his humble disciples so much that welcoming a humble disciple is equivalent

---

[1] Bonhoeffer, p. 184.
[2] 10:40 makes a similar point as 18:5. Mark 9:42–48 is a parallel passage to 18:5–14. Luke 15:4–7 is a parallel passage to 18:5–14 in a different setting.

to welcoming Jesus himself. The welcome is not just ordinary hospitality; it is hospitality given in Jesus' name.

> Don't neglect to show hospitality, for by doing this some have welcomed angels as guests without knowing it.
>
> Hebrews 13:2 (CSB)

When I am at a Christian event, I look over the crowd to find the shy inconspicuous brother and then make it my business to visit with him. It is more rewarding than trying to talk with the famous preacher who is the guest speaker. Though sometimes, it is the guest speaker who is lonely and appreciates simple friendship in Jesus' name.

Do not cause to stumble

I taught a class on how some people misuse and misinterpret the Scriptures. A new believer in the class was shocked by the idea Christian leaders misinterpret the Scriptures sometimes. I was glad he quickly dropped the class. He didn't need to delve into that topic at that time. He was still learning the Scriptures for the first time, building his faith, and growing in his relationship with the Lord.

Matthew 18:6–9 (CSB)[3]

---

6 But whoever causes one of these little ones who believe in me to fall away—it would be better for him if a heavy millstone were hung around his neck and he were drowned in the depths of the sea. 7 Woe to the world because of offenses. For offenses will inevitably come, but woe to that person by whom the offense comes.

8 If your hand or your foot causes you to fall away, cut it off and throw it away. It is better for you to enter life maimed or lame than to have two hands or two feet and be thrown into the eternal fire. 9 And if your eye causes you to fall away, gouge it out and throw it away. It is better for you to enter life with one eye than to have two eyes and be thrown into hellfire.

Jesus warned against attacking the faith of humble believers. It is better to enter the Kingdom of Heaven maimed than to face judgment for hindering a humble disciple. The illustration of cutting off a hand or foot or eye is obviously hyperbole, because everyone knows sinful actions are motivated by the heart, and the selfish desires of the soul lead one into temptation. The hand, foot, and eye do not have their own motivations.

---

[3] A *millstone* in verse 6 was a large stone pulled around by a donkey grinding grain, so one was sure to drown if it was around the neck.

Let us no longer judge one another. Instead decide never to put a stumbling block or pitfall in the way of your brother or sister.

Romans 14:13 (CSB)

The Father cares about the humble disciple so deeply that anyone who leads him astray will be punished severely. Sin is bad. Causing someone else to sin is double bad. Causing a humble disciple to sin is triple bad, deserving judgment by drowning in the sea. If my selfishness might cause a little one in the faith to stumble, then I must cleanse my life.

Do not despise

I taught a Bible school class at the college level. Two ladies in the class had only a fourth-grade education. I wondered how they would do. To my surprise, they did well on all the assignments and exams and made good contributions to class discussions. I had to repent of my doubts about them.

Matthew 18:10–11 (CSB)[4]

---

10 See to it that you don't despise one of these little ones, because I tell you that in heaven their angels continually view the face of my Father in heaven.

Even the most humble believer is very precious to the heavenly Father. Jesus warned us not to despise humble disciples. Spiritual pride which would elevate one believer over another is repugnant to God.

Accept anyone who is weak in faith, but don't argue about disputed matters... Who are you to judge another's household servant? Before his own Lord he stands or falls. And he will stand, because the Lord is able to make him stand...

But you, why do you judge your brother or sister? Or you, why do you despise your brother or sister? For we will all stand before the judgment seat of God.

Romans 14:1–10 (CSB)

Some Christians like to argue over their opinions and interpretations of Scriptures. It is usually not my job to straighten out warped theology, but sometimes I get drawn into a theology argument. I can afford to let the other person have the last word. I'm willing to let him disagree with my opinions. I will love him anyway. One of my favorite slogans is "It is better to be righteous than right."

---

[4]There are several possible interpretations of the word *angels* in verse 10 (Carson, pp. 400–401). The CSB omits verse 11 because its authenticity is debated by scholars, but the authenticity of Luke 19:10, which is practically the same, is accepted (Carson, p. 401).

The lost sheep

There was a fire drill at the day-care center. All the kids and the workers were out in the parking lot. The staff tried to get everyone to sit on the curb in a group. A curious little one went to investigate something over there. A worker had to run after him.

Matthew 18:12–14 (CSB)

---

12 What do you think? If someone has a hundred sheep, and one of them goes astray, won't he leave the ninety-nine on the hillside and go and search for the stray? 13 And if he finds it, truly I tell you, he rejoices over that sheep more than over the ninety-nine that did not go astray. 14 In the same way, it is not the will of your Father in heaven that one of these little ones perish.

The parable of the lost sheep illustrates the Father's love for each individual disciple. Even if a disciple is tempted and falls, the good shepherd seeks him out to restore him to the flock. This is personally applicable. If I should stumble, I know God will seek me out. He is always trying to restore the lost sheep, one by one.

[Jesus said:] I am the good shepherd. I know my own, and my own know me.

John 10:14 (CSB)

Jesus himself is the shepherd who looks for the lost lamb. We sometimes refer to the pastor of a church as a *shepherd*. He is responsible to care for the local sheep under the authority of the Good Shepherd. I like to refer to the leaders of small groups as *sheep dogs*, because they have close personal relationships with the group's individuals, and chase after strays.

Protect a child

Jesus protects the humble disciple like a parent protects a child, and I should do so as well. Jesus identifies with each humble disciple. Hospitality given in Jesus' name to a humble disciple is equivalent to welcoming Jesus himself. So, I will seek out the humble believer who is avoiding attention and make him feel welcome.

The heavenly Father loves the humble disciple so much that anyone who causes him to stumble will face severe punishment. I must be careful to cleanse my life of any selfishness that might cause others to sin. My pride would try to lift myself up over others, but Jesus sees the humble disciple as most important. I must repent of my pride and never denigrate a humble disciple.

The parable of the lost sheep shows how Jesus, the Good Shepherd, will seek out any disciple who strays from him, even the most insignificant one.

Jesus welcomes every humble believer and seeks to restore the one who strays. I will be careful not to cause the humble believer to stumble. I will honor the humble disciple.

19

Reconcile with your brother

There is therefore only one way of following Jesus and of worshipping God,
and that is to be reconciled with our brethren.

Dietrich Bonhoeffer[1]

Offenses between Christians disrupt worship and love for one another. Reconciliation is the only way to stay on the Kingdom path.

For example, Mark was a relative of Barnabus who accompanied Paul and Barnabus on their first missionary journey. He returned home part way through the trip. Paul was disappointed Mark did not complete the mission. Later, when planning another trip, Paul and Barnabus had a sharp disagreement over whether to take Mark. So, they went separate ways.[2] Evidently, Paul and Mark were reconciled, because later Mark was a valued coworker with Paul.[3]

Matthew 18:15–20 (CSB)

---

15 If your brother sins against you, go and rebuke him in private. If he listens to you, you have won your brother. 16 But if he won't listen, take one or two others with you, so that 'by the testimony of two or three witnesses every fact may be established.' 17 If he doesn't pay attention to them, tell the church. If he doesn't pay attention even to the church, let him be like a Gentile and a tax collector to you.

18 Truly I tell you, whatever you bind on earth will have been bound in heaven, and whatever you loose on earth will have been loosed in heaven.

19 Again, truly I tell you, if two of you on earth agree about any matter that you pray for, it will be done for you by my Father

---

[1] Bonhoeffer, p. 145.
[2] Acts 15:37–39.
[3] Colossians 4:10 and 2 Timothy 4:11.

in heaven. 20 For where two or three are gathered together in my name, I am there among them.

The context of this passage is about humility, so the one rebuking a brother must do so with a humble attitude, hoping for repentance and reconciliation.

Verse 18 begins, "Truly I tell you," (CSB) which implies the verse is continuing the message of reconciliation in verses 15 to 17.[4] Some Christians take verse 18 out of context and "bind" or "loose" whatever they please. That's probably not what Jesus had in mind.[5]

Verse 19 begins with, "Again, truly I tell you," (CSB) which implies verses 19 and 20 are continuing the same message even more. Some Christians take these verses out of context, thinking the "prayer of agreement" is a guarantee God will do whatever they want. There are many promises regarding prayer in the Bible, but that is probably not what Jesus meant here.

Reconcile

Two Christian friends were business partners. One used company funds for personal expenses. When confronted by her partner, she repented of the theft and made restitution. Their relationship was restored.

Paul instructed Timothy to balance rebuke and correction with encouragement, patience, and teaching.

> Preach the word; be ready in season and out of season; rebuke, correct, and encourage with great patience and teaching.
>
> 2 Timothy 4:2 (CSB)

The reconciliation process Jesus specified in 18:15–17 takes time and persistence. The process works, even in heart-wrenching situations. Discipline is necessary to protect other believers, but it is never easy for anyone involved. There is a special bond among believers and a special responsibility toward each other to be persistent, trying to reconcile the rebellious.

In modern society, almost all church meetings are open to the public. So, unbelievers are welcome. We too often forget not everyone in church is a believer, and not all believers are living the Kingdom lifestyle. This reconciliation process applies only to those who claim to be believers, and to those situations where one believer is victim of another's sin. The process is not applicable to non-Christians, even if they attend church.

Jesus said if the offender does not repent to treat him like a "Gentile and a tax collector" (CSB). A *Gentile* referred to a non-Jewish pagan, and a tax collector was regarded as the most immoral person in Jewish society, much like

---

[4]Jesus previously gave Peter similar authority regarding binding and loosing (16:19).
[5]Carson (pp. 372–374) argues, due to the context, *whatever* in 18:18 refers to the person being reconciled rather than things.

a corrupt bureaucrat. I can be friendly toward anyone, so I will still love the rebellious person who is under church discipline the same as I love other unbelievers.

Binding and loosing

In Paul's first letter to Christians in Corinth, he instructed them to discipline a man engaged in incest with his father's wife.[6]

> This punishment by the majority is sufficient for that person. As a result, you should instead forgive and comfort him. Otherwise, he may be overwhelmed by excessive grief. Therefore I urge you to reaffirm your love to him.
>
> 2 Corinthians 2:6–8 (CSB)

As a result of church discipline, the man engaged in incest repented. In his second letter, Paul told them to forgive and comfort him as a brother.

In the context of this chapter in Matthew, those under church discipline are the ones who are bound and loosed. The words *bound* and *loosed* correspond to the possible outcomes of the reconciliation process in the prior verses, either the offender is regarded as a disciple or is regarded as an unbeliever. This is confirmed in heaven, which implies God has given the body of Christ authority to administer discipline.

In agreement

When a fellow Christian refuses to repent, and thus, is regarded as an unbeliever, I will still be persistent in praying for him. It may take a while for him to come to his senses. God's grace never gives up, so I won't either.

> Rejoice in hope; be patient in affliction; be persistent in prayer.
>
> Romans 12:12 (CSB)

In the reconciliation process, there are two possible outcomes, either the offender is regarded as an unbeliever or he repents and is reconciled. The subject of agreement between two believers is the same two possible outcomes. When I am involved in church discipline, I will pray for the repentance and reconciliation of the offender and my prayer partner will agree with me. After reconciliation, the offender and the victim can pray together effectively as brothers.[7]

When Jesus is in their midst, believers will listen to and obey the Holy Spirit throughout the reconciliation process. The spiritual presence of Jesus reinforces their authority in administering discipline in a godly way.

---

[6]1 Corinthians 5:1–13.

[7]Carson (p. 403) suggests the two praying are the offender and the victim at the time of reconciliation.

Reconcile with your brother

Jesus emphasized the importance of reconciliation among believers. Pride is often the barrier between brothers, but the humble disciple will pursue reconciliation.

Jesus prescribed a persistent step-by-step process for reconciliation when a fellow believer sins against me. The process takes time. Sin may have heart-wrenching consequences, but I will be persistent.

The reconciliation process may result in restoration or a broken relationship. The words *bound* and *loosed* correspond to these possibilities. God has given the body of Christ authority for administering this reconciliation process. When believers pray through a reconciliation situation, Jesus is spiritually present and will work in that situation. After reconciliation, effective prayer as brothers becomes possible.

When one believer offends another, they are not alone to resolve their differences. Other believers can help in the reconciliation process. They have authority over the outcome. They will pray together for resolution and restoration. Humble disciples will reconcile with each other whenever there is an offense.

20

Forgive your brother

The passion of Christ strengthens [a disciple] to overcome the sins of others by forgiving them. He becomes the bearer of other men's burdens.[1] As Christ bears our burdens, so ought we to bear the burdens of our fellow-men...And the only way to bear that sin is by forgiving it in the power of the cross of Christ in which [we] now share.

Dietrich Bonhoeffer[2]

Bonhoeffer was arrested by the Nazi Gestapo. He endured constant interrogation and mistreatment until his execution about two years later. He was prepared to forgive his captors over and over, day after day.

How many times?

I like to play ping pong.[3] First, I hit a forehand and then a backhand, and then I lunge for the corner of the table. When you slam the ball toward me, it seems to be coming at 90 miles per hour. If I'm to have any hope of hitting it back to you, I must be quick. Forgiveness requires quick reactions, too.

Matthew 18:21–22 (CSB)

---

21 Then Peter approached him and asked, "Lord, how many times shall I forgive my brother or sister who sins against me? As many as seven times?"

22 "I tell you, not as many as seven," Jesus replied, "but seventy times seven."

---

[1] Galatians 6:2.
[2] Bonhoeffer, p. 100.
[3] Table tennis.

I'm sure I would lose count if I tried to keep track of offenses. *Seventy times seven*[4] means such a big number that I must forgive indefinitely.

> Therefore, as God's chosen ones, holy and dearly loved, put on compassion, kindness, humility, gentleness, and patience, bearing with one another and forgiving one another if anyone has a grievance against another. Just as the Lord has forgiven you, so you are also to forgive. Above all, put on love, which is the perfect bond of unity.
>
> Colossians 3:12–14 (CSB)

I have tendency to speak when someone else is talking. It has been a lifelong inconsiderate habit. My wife corrects me with love and gentleness. I'm learning to notice her signals when we are in a group conversation. I need her forgiveness.

Throughout life there are plenty of opportunities to take offense, get mad, and become bitter. Children disrespect their elders. Adults insult each other. One might be the victim of betrayal, cheating, white collar crime, violent crime, or government injustice. All of us have excuses to cling to unforgiveness.

Jesus taught us to pray, "Forgive us our debts as we also have forgiven our debtors."[5] Forgiving others over and over is part of the Kingdom lifestyle. My forgiving is not conditional on the offender's apology or repentance. I must forgive as soon as I notice I feel wounded or offended.

Only after I have forgiven am I qualified to follow up on the situation in a godly way. Parents may need to discipline their children as godly teachers. A judge or parent may have to administer justice. I may need to take steps to protect myself from future abuse, crime, or injustice. I may need to seek restitution of what was stolen. It is not my job to get revenge. That is God's job.[6] If I have not forgiven, then my attitude is corrupted when I try to follow up on the situation.

My policy is to immediately forgive every hurt, every unkind word, every mistake, every selfish reaction. This is expressed by acts of kindness and compassion for the one who hurt me.[7] I am learning to be an instant forgiver, so I can forgive over and over. Seventy times seven offenses per person per day is too many for me to keep count.

The unmerciful servant

After telling Peter to forgive, Jesus illustrated his point with the parable of the unforgiving servant. The humble disciple must forgive.

---

[4] The Greek expression translated *seventy times seven* by the CSB in 18:22 is ambiguous. Some translations prefer *seventy-seven* (Carson, p. 405).

[5] 6:12 (CSB).

[6] Romans 12:19.

[7] 1 Peter 3:8–9.

Matthew 18:23–35 (CSB)

---

23 For this reason, the kingdom of heaven can be compared to a king who wanted to settle accounts with his servants. 24 When he began to settle accounts, one who owed ten thousand talents was brought before him. 25 Since he did not have the money to pay it back, his master commanded that he, his wife, his children, and everything he had be sold to pay the debt.

26 At this, the servant fell facedown before him and said, 'Be patient with me, and I will pay you everything.' 27 Then the master of that servant had compassion, released him, and forgave him the loan.

28 That servant went out and found one of his fellow servants who owed him a hundred denarii. He grabbed him, started choking him, and said, 'Pay what you owe!'

29 At this, his fellow servant fell down and began begging him, 'Be patient with me, and I will pay you back.' 30 But he wasn't willing. Instead, he went and threw him into prison until he could pay what was owed. 31 When the other servants saw what had taken place, they were deeply distressed and went and reported to their master everything that had happened.

32 Then, after he had summoned him, his master said to him, 'You wicked servant! I forgave you all that debt because you begged me. 33 Shouldn't you also have had mercy on your fellow servant, as I had mercy on you?' 34 And because he was angry, his master handed him over to the jailers to be tortured until he could pay everything that was owed. 35 So also my heavenly Father will do to you unless every one of you forgives his brother or sister from your heart.

A *talent* in ancient times was a measure of weight for various metals and later a measure of coinage. Some estimate the value of a talent of silver in Roman times to be about 6,000 *denarii* where a *denarius* was a day's wage for a laborer.[8] In modern terms, one talent would be worth 6,000 times the minimum wage for a day's work. The unmerciful servant's debt was 10,000 talents, so his debt was astronomical—just like my sins.

> [God] made you alive with him and forgave us all our trespasses. He erased the certificate of debt, with its obligations, that was against us and opposed to us, and has taken it away by nailing it to the cross.
>
> Colossians 2:13–14 (CSB)

My father loaned a friend several thousand dollars. After my father died, I was responsible for collecting the debt. Later, the friend declared bankruptcy

---

[8]Carson, p. 516.

and could not pay it back, so the debt was legally canceled. I was faced with a choice: would I forgive the debt in my heart or would I become bitter? I sent him a note confirming that I forgave the debt, too.

Holding unforgiveness is unhealthy for me. It is not revenge for the offense. Usually the offender does not care who got hurt or how they feel. The offender just goes on his way. My unforgiveness does not affect the offender. It only affects me. Unforgiveness robs me of peace, joy, fellowship with the Father, and a multitude of other Kingdom blessings. Why should I hold on to it?

The great debt of the unmerciful servant is like the great debt of my sin. Jesus died to pay that debt. The debt of the fellow slave corresponds to wounds I might suffer in life. The debt of my sin before God is astronomical compared to being a victim of another person's sin.

The lesson of the story is clear. Unforgiveness is such a great evil the heavenly Father will be like the king in the story, severely punishing those who do not forgive. Because I have been forgiven of a great debt, I must forgive others whenever they hurt me.

Forgive your brother

Peter thought forgiving seven times was plenty, but Jesus showed him what the heavenly Father thinks about forgiveness. My forgiving does not require an apology from the other person. I must forgive unconditionally like God has forgiven me. I am becoming a quick forgiver, so seventy times seven offenses won't seem like many.

The parable of the unmerciful servant illustrates how unforgiveness is a great evil. I have been forgiven much by God, so I must forgive others whenever I am offended. The humble disciple is always ready to forgive.

21

Greatest in the Kingdom

For the only honour and dignity [the disciples] know is their Lord's own mercy, to which alone they owe their very lives.

Dietrich Bonhoeffer[1]

The disciples started this discourse by asking "Who is greatest in the Kingdom of Heaven?" Jesus answered the question directly and then proceeded to explain the characteristics of the greatest disciple.

Who is the greatest?   The humble disciple is the greatest in the Kingdom of Heaven. Jesus illustrated his point with a small child. A disciple must be humble like a small child.

Protect a child. Not only is the humble disciple great, but he deserves protection. One must be careful not to cause the humble disciple to sin. The parable of the lost sheep illustrates how the Jesus, the Good Shepherd, seeks out the wandering disciple like a shepherd seeks the lost sheep.

Reconcile with your brother. A humble disciple seeks reconciliation with a brother who sins against him. The reconciliation process starts in private, but other believers are available to help resolve the situation.

Forgive your brother. A humble disciple is quick to forgive a brother who sins against him over and over, because he has been forgiven much by the heavenly Father.

The greatest in the Kingdom. My goal is to be like that humble disciple who honors others above himself. I will protect those who are new in the faith. I will be eager to reconcile with my brothers. I will forgive over and over.

---

[1]Bonhoeffer, p. 125.

Part V

The coming of the king

22

The return of Jesus

The Church has never forgotten Christ's promise of his imminent return, and she has always believed that this promise is true.

Dietrich Bonhoeffer[1]

Imminent means an event could happen at any moment. Christians have been eager to see Jesus return ever since he ascended into the sky. I'm eager, too. The darker society becomes, the more I look for him. His return could be at any moment. The king's coming is imminent.

Whenever Queen Elizabeth of England visits Canada, where she is monarch and head of state, elaborate preparations are made to honor her arrival.[2] An advance team choreographs each step of the visit. The day and time of her arrival is set. Transportation is provided. Crowds gather to see her. Her agenda is carefully followed. She receives diplomatic protocol honors. She wields constitutional royal authority.

The coming of King Jesus will begin his reign over all the nations of the world with all power and authority. Even the Queen of England will submit to his authority.

Christians have many interpretations of details about the return of Jesus. As a result, there is a wide variety of interpretations of this discourse. Commentators try to fit the discourse's details into their ideas about his return. Most agree on these basic points.

- Jesus will personally return.

- Believers will rise from the dead to eternal life.

- Unbelievers will face eternal judgment.

---

[1] Bonhoeffer, p. 239.

[2] The Queen of England is also the head of the Commonwealth of Nations, which is composed of over 50 countries most of which were formerly territories of the British Empire. The Queen is monarch and head of state of sixteen of these member states.

- Expect him soon!

These points are directly supported by other Scriptures. In this book, I emphasize these points and ignore many details about Jesus' return. Our goal here is to draw devotional thoughts from each passage in the discourse, so everyone can benefit from this discourse without being distracted by controversies.[3]

Jesus will personally return

The fire-drill bell sounded. Everyone in class marched outside. Then we watched a small flame rise from the horizon into the sky and disappear. John Glenn had just become America's first man to orbit Planet Earth. I stood there in awe.

The following verses describe what happened when Jesus ascended into the sky after his resurrection.

> After [Jesus] had said this, he was taken up as [the disciples] were watching, and a cloud took him out of their sight. While he was going, they were gazing into heaven, and suddenly two men in white clothes stood by them. They said, "Men of Galilee, why do you stand looking up into heaven? This same Jesus, who has been taken from you into heaven, will come in the same way that you have seen him going into heaven."
>
> Acts 1:9–11 (CSB)

While the disciples were standing there in awe, the angels spoke to them and explicitly said Jesus will come again. The disciples' personal contact with Jesus was comforting. His leaving earth must have been disappointing. However, Jesus promised the Holy Spirit,[4] so millions of us can experience his presence while we wait for his return. Jesus will personally return to Planet Earth.

Believers will rise from the dead

Whenever I attend the funeral of a believer, I grieve over the loss of fellowship in this life, but I am comforted by the hope of eternal life together. When the casket is lowered into the grave, I know the dead body will decompose, but I am comforted by the hope of resurrected bodies, because Jesus has a resurrected body.

Paul explained to the Thessalonians what will happen to us who believe when Jesus returns.

---

[3]Many commentators also rely on the book of Revelation for details about Jesus' return. My book, *Revelation: A Devotional Commentary*, emphasizes the above basic points while presenting devotional applications. Edward B. Allen, *Revelation: A Devotional Commentary* (Melbourne, Florida: Edward B. Allen, 2016).

[4]John 14:25–27.

> We do not want you to be uninformed, brothers and sisters, concerning those who are asleep, so that you will not grieve like the rest, who have no hope. For if we believe that Jesus died and rose again, in the same way, through Jesus, God will bring with him those who have fallen asleep. For we say this to you by a word from the Lord: We who are still alive at the Lord's coming will certainly not precede those who have fallen asleep. For the Lord himself will descend from heaven with a shout, with the archangel's voice, and with the trumpet of God, and the dead in Christ will rise first. Then we who are still alive, who are left, will be caught up together with them in the clouds to meet the Lord in the air, and so we will always be with the Lord. Therefore encourage one another with these words.
>
> 1 Thessalonians 4:13–18 (CSB)

Jesus said believers will be gathered from throughout the world.[5] Believers who have died will rise from the dead when Jesus returns, and those believers who are alive at that time will also be caught up to meet the Lord. Paul ends these verses with the promise, "So we will always be with the Lord."

Paul similarly encouraged the Corinthians. Believers will receive immortal bodies at their resurrection.[6] Sin and death will be defeated. The resurrection of Jesus was the guarantee of his complete victory.[7] My hope for eternal life is founded on the reality of Jesus' resurrection. His promise that I will be resurrected is backed up by the fact he is alive now.[8] Believers will rise from the dead to eternal life.

Unbelievers will face eternal judgment

Benjamin Franklin wrote to a friend, "In this world, nothing can be said to be certain, except death and taxes." He forgot to mention unbelievers will face judgment after Jesus returns.

> Because of your hardened and unrepentant heart you are storing up wrath for yourself in the day of wrath, when God's righteous judgment is revealed. He will repay each one according to his works: eternal life to those who by persistence in doing good seek glory, honor, and immortality; but wrath and anger to those who are self-seeking and disobey the truth while obeying unrighteousness.
>
> Romans 2:5–8 (CSB)

---

[5] 24:31.
[6] 1 Corinthians 15:51–57.
[7] Romans 6:5 and 1 Peter 1:3.
[8] John 14:19.

Everyone will face judgment.[9] Believers will be saved by faith,[10] which results in good works. Unbelievers will face judgment for their unrighteous works.

The prospect of eternal torment is pretty scary. When I heard about God's plan for salvation, I was eager to believe, to accept it, and to begin a life of discipleship, instead of rebelling against God. Unbelievers will face eternal judgment.

Expect him soon

When I was a teenager, I read all the books I could find about the return of Jesus. I tried to learn all about it. Is Jesus coming soon? Will he come within my lifetime? Can I discern the "signs of the times"?

> He who testifies about these things says, "Yes, I am coming soon."
> Amen! Come, Lord Jesus!
>
> Revelation 22:20 (CSB)

Jesus said one cannot know the day of his return, but believers must be ready for his return at any time.[11] When he arrives, I should be doing what he has directed me to do. I'm concentrating on living the Kingdom lifestyle now with eager anticipation. Expect him soon!

---

[9]Hebrews 9:27.
[10]Romans 3:22–24.
[11]24:42–44.

23

Before his coming

Until now the world had always granted [Christians] a lodging-place by allowing them to work for their own food and clothing. But a world that has become one hundred percent anti-Christian cannot allow them even this private sphere of work for their daily bread...When the Christian community has been deprived of its last inch of space on earth, the end will be near.

Dietrich Bonhoeffer[1]

Bonhoeffer published *The Cost of Discipleship* in 1937 as Hitler tightened his grip on Germany. Bonhoeffer foresaw how those following Jesus would soon be persecuted by the Nazi regime. In the twenty-first century, persecution is happening around the world on an even larger scale. Bonhoeffer predicted when Christians are evicted from their ability to make a living by the world system, Jesus will come.

Birth pains

A pregnant woman's contractions prior to delivery are a sign of a coming event, not the event itself. The "labor pains"[2] Jesus talked about are signs that Jesus is coming, but not the event itself.

Matthew 24:1–8 (CSB)

---

1 As Jesus left and was going out of the temple, his disciples came up and called his attention to its buildings. 2 He replied to them, "Do you see all these things? Truly I tell you, not one stone will be left here on another that will not be thrown down."

---

[1]Bonhoeffer, pp. 299–300.
[2]24:8 (CSB).

3 While he was sitting on the Mount of Olives, the disciples approached him privately and said, "Tell us, when will these things happen? And what is the sign of your coming and of the end of the age?"

4 Jesus replied to them: "Watch out that no one deceives you. 5 For many will come in my name, saying, 'I am the Messiah,' and they will deceive many. 6 You are going to hear of wars and rumors of wars. See that you are not alarmed, because these things must take place, but the end is not yet. 7 For nation will rise up against nation, and kingdom against kingdom. There will be famines and earthquakes in various places. 8 All these events are the beginning of labor pains."

Matthew 24 and 25 is called the *Olivet Discourse*, because Jesus was sitting on the Mount of Olives when he spoke. While in the neighborhood of the temple, Jesus remarked that the temple would be completely destroyed. The disciples later asked these linked questions.

- When will the temple be destroyed?

- What will be the sign of your coming as Messiah?

- What will be the sign of the end of the age?

This discourse addresses these questions, but not in the way the disciples expected. They were hoping for him to begin his reign immediately. The temple was destroyed in AD 70 by the Romans after a siege of Jerusalem, fulfilling Jesus' prophecy. Jesus explained some things that must happen before he returns. Finally, his coming will mark the end of this current imperfect age. The coming of Jesus, the Messiah, to rule as king on earth will complete the coming of the Kingdom of Heaven.

Jesus warned about chaotic conditions prior to his return, such as false messiahs, wars, conflicts, famines, and earthquakes.

> Evil people and impostors will become worse, deceiving and being deceived. But as for you, continue in what you have learned and firmly believed.
>
> 2 Timothy 3:13–14 (CSB)

The guys at the Bible study seemed to be in awe of a certain Bible teacher on television. They passed around his newsletter hoping everyone would sign up. His newsletter emphasized minor points about the return of Jesus and outrage over current events. I decided to just focus on the basics of Kingdom living instead.

From time to time, we read in the news about a cult where a leader with a strong personality manipulates his flock. They follow in blind obedience. Such extreme cases are obviously false messiahs. However, it is more common for

Christians to lift up some leader and hang on every word, written or spoken. The leader may be a famous pastor, evangelist, author, or television personality. He never claims to be the Christ, but people treat him like a messiah.

Such a situation is not Kingdom living under the lordship of Jesus. Jesus told us not to be deceived. I will avoid giving praise to men that belongs to God.

The turmoil Jesus described is intimidating. Will God still be in control? Will he still love me?

> Who can separate us from the love of Christ? Can affliction or distress or persecution or famine or nakedness or danger or sword?
> Romans 8:35 (CSB)

Wars and fears of wars have been common throughout the twentieth and twenty-first centuries, both hot wars and cold wars. Ethnic groups have tried to wipe each other out. Nation states have grappled with each other for advantage. Terrorists have waged war beyond nation-state boundaries. This turmoil has caused famines among those caught in war zones. Urbanization has magnified the impact of earthquakes on people. Such events guarantee Jesus is coming.

Through all the difficulties and turmoil before Jesus returns, God's love for me is unshakable.[3] His love will comfort me even if I am caught up in wars, conflicts, famines, or earthquakes.

Endure

Mike ran in the Chicago Marathon. Even though it may not have been comfortable, he trained for the event to build up his endurance. To finish the race, he pressed on mile after mile. He endured to the end.

Matthew 24:9–13 (CSB)

---

9 Then they will hand you over to be persecuted, and they will kill you. You will be hated by all nations because of my name. 10 Then many will fall away, betray one another, and hate one another. 11 Many false prophets will rise up and deceive many. 12 Because lawlessness will multiply, the love of many will grow cold. 13 But the one who endures to the end will be saved.

Jesus had already warned the apostles of persecution when he sent them on a mission.[4] He reemphasized that message here.

---

[3]Romans 8:37–39.
[4]10:16–25.

[Jesus said:] If the world hates you, understand that it hated me before it hated you. If you were of the world, the world would love you as its own. However, because you are not of the world, but I have chosen you out of it, the world hates you.

John 15:18–19 (CSB)

While the birth pains have progressed, Christians have been persecuted, and even put to death. This has been happening ever since the first century at various times in various places.

In the twentieth century, communism was the major persecutor of the Kingdom. The collapse of the Soviet Union ushered in wide spread proclamation of the gospel there. In spite of persecution by the communists, China has experienced the greatest growth of the church in history. The growth has been indigenous with little involvement by the modern Western missionary movement.

In the twenty-first century, Islam has a renewed hostility toward the Kingdom and anything bearing the name of Christ. During war with the Islamic State, Christians whose forefathers had lived in Iraq for centuries were forced to flee or face genocide.[5]

In twenty-first-century America, the hostility of the political left toward the Kingdom has grown more and more rabid. On the surface, the political left appears to be a mosaic of special interest groups, such as socialists, homosexuals, abortion advocates, and atheists, but they are bound together by hostility toward the teachings of the Bible and toward Christ. Wherever the left gains political power, persecution of Christians follows in venues small and large.

Even the institutional church will be affected. Some will fall away from the truth of the Bible and follow false teachers.

There were indeed false prophets among the people, just as there will be false teachers among you. They will bring in destructive heresies, even denying the Master who bought them, and will bring swift destruction on themselves.

2 Peter 2:1 (CSB)

Whenever I eat barbecue spare ribs, I must use my hands. A knife and fork won't work. I gnaw the meat from the bone. The bones pile up, destined for the trash. False teaching is like bones destined for the trash.

Throughout church history there have been famous teachers who have led some of God's people astray. They often added unbiblical practices and traditions to the gospel.

Anyone can have mistaken doctrinal ideas, even famous respected teachers. True humble followers of Jesus will always be open to correction from the Word of God. Whenever I listen to Christian teachers, I eat the meat and throw away the bones.

---

[5]"Iraq Christians flee as Islamic State takes Qaraqosh," *BBC News*, Augusts 7, 2014. Available at https://www.bbc.com/news/world-middle-east-28686998 (Current March 1, 2019).

But know this: Hard times will come in the last days. For people will be lovers of self, lovers of money, boastful, proud, demeaning, disobedient to parents, ungrateful, unholy, unloving, irreconcilable, slanderers, without self-control, brutal, without love for what is good, traitors, reckless, conceited, lovers of pleasure rather than lovers of God, holding to the form of godliness but denying its power. Avoid these people.

2 Timothy 3:1–5 (CSB)

Many city dwellers are facing increasing crime and violence, disrespect for authority, foul profane speech, garbage on the streets, and reckless drivers. Trends of increased lawlessness and cold hearts are evident in modern society.

The same trends are seen in the institutional church as well. I have visited churches that do not teach the Kingdom message, where people attend but don't have faith, where people follow their own ideas in daily life instead of Kingdom living, and where selfishness reigns instead of love for God and love for neighbor. When people do as they please, lawlessness abounds, love grows cold, and loyal disciples suffer.

We also rejoice in our afflictions, because we know that affliction produces endurance, endurance produces proven character, and proven character produces hope. This hope will not disappoint us, because God's love has been poured out in our hearts through the Holy Spirit who was given to us.

Romans 5:3–5 (CSB)

At basketball practice, the players ran from sideline to sideline until they were exhausted, and then they practiced making foul shots. How can anyone hope to throw the ball through the hoop when exhausted? But that is what the coach demanded. They built up their endurance at practice, so they would be ready for the game on Saturday.

Even though the institutional church may be corrupted during times of birth pains, God's plan cannot be derailed by the weakness of churchmen. Jesus promised, "The one who endures to the end will be saved."[6] I will persevere through persecution, hatred, and deception. Turmoil, false teachers, and lawlessness are signs that Jesus' return is guaranteed.

The gospel preached

The spread of the gospel in China during my lifetime has amazed me. Western missionaries were expelled after the communists came to power in 1949. The communist state mercilessly persecuted, jailed, and killed Christians. Yet the gospel kept spreading. Much of what Christians did was hidden due to the persecution. In the 1990s and 2000s, the persecution lessened in some places. The rest of the world gradually learned millions had converted to Christianity.

---

[6]24:13 (CSB).

Matthew 24:14 (CSB)

---

14 This good news of the kingdom will be proclaimed in all the world as a testimony to all nations, and then the end will come.

The Great Commission[7] sent Jesus' followers all over the world. Verse 14 above indicates why Jesus did so—to proclaim the gospel to all kinds of people before he returns.

> The Lord does not delay his promise, as some understand delay, but is patient with you, not wanting any to perish but all to come to repentance.
>
>   2 Peter 3:9 (CSB)

The spread of the gospel today is taking advantage of modern technologies like radio, television, and the Internet. Bible translators are rapidly making the Word of God available in the heart-languages of millions. Indigenous missionaries are reaching people in remote areas of their own countries.

Jesus promised he will return to establish the Kingdom of Heaven on earth, but before that happens, God is giving people ample opportunity to repent. The disciples hoped Jesus would set up his Kingdom immediately, but God's plan included work for us to do first.

Flee

If you live close to the ocean when a hurricane is coming, you must evacuate to a safer place inland. Hurricanes often bring exceptionally high tides and destructive surf which flood the land. When danger is coming, fleeing is the prudent thing to do.

Matthew 24:15–22 (CSB)

---

15 "So when you see the abomination of desolation, spoken of by the prophet Daniel, standing in the holy place" (let the reader understand), 16 "then those in Judea must flee to the mountains. 17 A man on the housetop must not come down to get things out of his house, 18 and a man in the field must not go back to get his coat. 19 Woe to pregnant women and nursing mothers in those days! 20 Pray that your escape may not be in winter or on a Sabbath. 21 For at that time there will be great distress, the kind that hasn't taken place from the beginning of the world until now and never will again. 22 Unless those days were cut short, no one would be saved. But those days will be cut short because of the elect."

---

[7]28:18–20.

It is not clear what *abomination* Jesus was referring to in this passage. Commentators have many theories about what Jesus meant by *abomination*,[8] but interpreting Daniel's prophecies is beyond the scope of this book.

> Come out of her, my people,
> so that you will not share in her sins
> or receive any of her plagues.
>
> Revelation 18:4 (CSB)

John's vision in Revelation warned believers to flee the desolation of the corrupt city he called *Babylon*. Similarly, Jesus advised believers in Judea to flee when they see desolation coming. This general advice was directly applicable to the siege of Jerusalem. Christian tradition indicates the Christians fled the city in about AD 68, about halfway through the siege.[9] Perhaps the Christians in Jerusalem interpreted some event as a sign that they should flee the besieged city, according to Jesus' admonition. Historians don't know. Instead of straining over history, let us apply the general message to today.

Throughout church history, the same advice was applicable to other periods of great distress. Even if modern events are not desecration of the temple in Jerusalem, if one sees an "abomination," one can be sure desolation is close behind. Fleeing the resulting great distress is the prudent thing to do.

> After this I looked, and there was a vast multitude from every nation, tribe, people, and language, which no one could number, standing before the throne and before the Lamb...
>
> These are the ones coming out of the great tribulation. They washed their robes and made them white in the blood of the Lamb.
>
> Revelation 7:9–14 (CSB)

In his vision, John saw a multitude of believers from every kind of background who had been through great distress. They were praising God before his throne. Jesus promised the duration of distress would be short.

Whenever I am going through distress, I am confident God is concerned for me. I also know believers through the centuries have experienced much worse distress than I ever will, and they were victorious. Therefore, I can be victorious, too.

Before his coming

The disciples asked Jesus, "What is the sign of your coming and of the end of the age?"[10] Everyone is curious about when the big event is coming. The disciples were probably disappointed so much needed to happen before Jesus

---

[8]Carson, p. 500.
[9]Carson, p. 501.
[10]24:3 (CSB).

begins to reign as king. Difficult times, persecution, and desolation must come first, as well as spreading the gospel.

Jesus warned his disciples of the chaotic times ahead. False messiahs will deceive many. Birth-pain events will cause great suffering. Persecution must be endured. Sometimes the distress will be so great that the prudent choice is to flee. Through all of this, the Kingdom message will be preached everywhere.

Birth pains. Jesus told the disciples he was not setting up his Kingdom on earth yet. Indeed, deception, wars, ethnic conflicts, famines, and earthquakes have razed the earth at various times and in various places ever since the first century, just as Jesus said.

Endure. Jesus explained the difficulties believers, in particular, will face. The Lord will deliver the ones who persevere. I must remain faithful to the Lord through persecution, hatred, deception, and lawlessness.

The gospel preached. God planned for all kinds of people to be in his Kingdom, so Jesus sent his disciples everywhere. Jesus promised to return after the Kingdom message has been preached in all the world.

Flee. When one sees abomination against the Lord and the great distress of desolation close behind, it is prudent to flee. I know God cares for me and he will carry me through distress like he has believers through the centuries.

Before his coming. While the Kingdom message is spreading, turmoil, persecution, and great distress all guarantee Jesus will return to establish the Kingdom of Heaven.

24

His coming

[Jesus has] the kingdom and the power and the glory for ever and ever in the unity of the Father. That is the assurance the disciples have.

Dietrich Bonhoeffer[1]

When Jesus returns to reign over all of Planet Earth, he will have all the power and glory that belongs to the rightful king of the universe. The doxology at the end of the Lord's Prayer says, "For thine is the kingdom, and the power, and the glory, for ever."[2] Christians have the assurance his authority is above all.

Not like false messiahs

False messiahs and false prophets try to get big crowds to show up for their conferences and special church services. We see their fliers and billboards all over town. Jesus won't need any advertising when he returns.

Matthew 24:23–28 (CSB)

---

23 If anyone tells you then, 'See, here is the Messiah!' or, 'Over here!' do not believe it. 24 For false messiahs and false prophets will arise and perform great signs and wonders to lead astray, if possible, even the elect. 25 Take note: I have told you in advance. 26 So if they tell you, 'See, he's in the wilderness!' don't go out; or, 'See, he's in the storerooms!' do not believe it. 27 For as the lightning comes from the east and flashes as far as the west, so will be the coming of the Son of Man. 28 Wherever the carcass is, there the vultures will gather.

---

[1] Bonhoeffer, p. 187.
[2] 6:13 (KJV).

Jesus warned his disciples not to chase after stories of his coming in this place or that. His coming will be obvious to everyone.

> Now some of the itinerant Jewish exorcists also attempted to pronounce the name of the Lord Jesus over those who had evil spirits, saying, "I command you by the Jesus that Paul preaches!" Seven sons of Sceva, a Jewish high priest, were doing this. The evil spirit answered them, "I know Jesus, and I recognize Paul—but who are you?"
>
> Acts 19:13–15 (CSB)

Apparently, the seven sons of Sceva successfully cast out demons. If they were doing this today, they would be famous. They might be on television. However, when they tried to use the authority of Jesus the Messiah, the demon said, "Who are you?"

Many people assume anyone who performs miracles has been endorsed by God. Jesus warned even deceivers can do miracles. Some sincere Christians go from one conference to another hoping to witness miracles for themselves. Similarly, if a guest speaker at church was involved in a miracle in the past, people from other churches in the community will flock to see the visitor. Too often Christians are gullible and easily deceived. The extreme case is when the deceiver claims to be a messiah himself. Signs, wonders, and miracles do not mean someone is endorsed by God.

Earlier in this discourse, Jesus warned his disciples against false messiahs and false prophets. He again warned that false messiahs will come. False messiahs may come to a remote place or a convention hall to meet with their followers, but when Jesus returns, it will be obvious to all. Jesus' return will not be done secretly.

> His lightning lights up the world;
> the earth sees and trembles.
> The mountains melt like wax
> at the presence of the Lord—
> at the presence of the Lord of the whole earth.
> The heavens proclaim his righteousness;
> all the peoples see his glory.
>
> Psalm 97:4–6 (CSB)

The night sky lit up as a thunderstorm rolled in. Everyone in town could see the cloud-to-cloud lightning stretched across the sky. The cloud-to-ground lightning crashed nearby and an electrical transformer threw sparks in the air.

Jesus explained why special discernment will not be needed to figure out whether the Messiah has come. It will be obvious to everyone like a flash of lightning. Jesus reinforced the point by comparing the sign of his coming to vultures in the sky which are a clear sign of a carcass. His coming will be just as obvious.

I ignore reports of some secret visitation. I can relax, knowing Jesus' return will be clear. No one will have doubts. I'm eager to see Jesus return as king to reign over this old earth, but I'm not gullible.

In the sky

The skywriter's plane buzzed overhead. Everyone wondered what the message would be. Letter by letter his smoke formed a word in the sky. Jesus' arrival will be seen in the sky. Everyone will find out he is king.

Matthew 24:29–31 (CSB)

---

29 Immediately after the distress of those days, the sun will be darkened, and the moon will not shed its light; the stars will fall from the sky, and the powers of the heavens will be shaken. 30 Then the sign of the Son of Man will appear in the sky, and then all the peoples of the earth will mourn; and they will see the Son of Man coming on the clouds of heaven with power and great glory. 31 He will send out his angels with a loud trumpet, and they will gather his elect from the four winds, from one end of the sky to the other.

When Jesus returns there will be signs in the sky such as the sun, moon, and stars going dark. The Greek word translated *sign* in verse 30 commonly meant the ensign or banner of a military leader.[3] His banner in the sky will announce his coming, and then he will be visible in the sky.

Look, the day of the Lord is coming—
cruel, with rage and burning anger—
to make the earth a desolation
and to destroy its sinners.
Indeed, the stars of the sky and its constellations
will not give their light.
The sun will be dark when it rises,
and the moon will not shine.

Isaiah 13:9–10 (CSB)

For thousands of years, mariners have used the sun, moon, and stars to navigate the seas. Similarly, Bedouins have used them to navigate in the desert. They entrusted their lives to the heavenly bodies, because their paths in the sky were always the same.

The motions of the sun, moon, and stars are among the most reliable things in life. By going dark, heavenly bodies will be signs of the king's imminent coming. People will realize how unreliable their lives are. His judgment on sin will change everything.

---

[3]The Greek word *semeion* (*Strong's* No. 4592). Carson, p. 505.

Celestial events today remind me of Jesus' promise. A solar eclipse blocks the sun. A lunar eclipse makes the moon look like blood. A meteor shower looks like stars falling from the sky. Ash from a volcano can circle the globe, blocking the sky. When I see these natural events, I remember that Jesus is coming.

> This same Jesus, who has been taken from you into heaven, will come in the same way that you have seen him going into heaven.
> Acts 1:11 (CSB)

I can imagine how people on earth will react when Jesus appears in the sky.[4] Military jets will scramble to investigate. They will see his power and glory. They'll take pictures. The news media will flash the pictures around the world. Everyone will hear about this strange phenomenon in the sky. The United Nations Security Council will call an emergency meeting to decide how to respond. After resolutions, press conferences, and communiques, they will send a military force which will be defeated. When Jesus takes his seat to rule, he will send a message to the United Nations General Assembly, "You can go home now. Your services are no longer needed."

> For the Lord himself will descend from heaven with a shout, with the archangel's voice, and with the trumpet of God, and the dead in Christ will rise first. Then we who are still alive, who are left, will be caught up together with them in the clouds to meet the Lord in the air, and so we will always be with the Lord.
> 1 Thessalonians 4:16–17 (CSB)

When the car drove into the driveway, little Mike ran outside. He was greeted by his uncle with a big hug. Mike's feet left the ground as his uncle swung him around in the air.

When Jesus returns, believers will have a reunion party. Our feet will leave the ground and we will be gathered together. We, the elect, will be changed and will be with the Lord forever.[5]

His coming

The kids were talking, arguing, poking each other, throwing wads of paper, and generally creating chaos, until the teacher came in and said, "Class!"

After all the prior turmoil, Jesus' return will bring relief. His reign will bring peace and order to this old world.

Not like false messiahs. Jesus' return will be clear. False messiahs may have secret meetings of the faithful, but I'm not gullible. There will be no doubt who Jesus is when he returns.

---

[4]Psalm 2:1–3.
[5]1 Corinthians 15:51–57.

In the sky. The sun, moon, and stars will indicate Jesus' return is imminent. Their going dark will shake everyone's sense of security. When Jesus appears in the sky, the leaders of the earth will think it is a crisis, but believers will know his reign will bring justice and righteousness.

His coming. Even though false messiahs may come and go, I know who the real Messiah is. His coming will be obvious. He will appear in the sky for all to see, and believers will be with the him forever.

25

When is he coming?

This much is clear and all-important for us today: that the return of Jesus will take place suddenly.

Dietrich Bonhoeffer[1]

When will Jesus the king come to reign on earth? Commentators have many interpretations of Bible prophecies. The details are interesting, but I will focus on this conclusion: as Bonhoeffer said, he will come suddenly, so I must always be ready.

A fig tree

The two mango trees in my backyard flower in the spring. When I see the little flowers, I know there will be mangoes in two or three months.

Matthew 24:32–35 (CSB)

---

32 Learn this lesson from the fig tree: As soon as its branch becomes tender and sprouts leaves, you know that summer is near. 33 In the same way, when you see all these things, recognize that he is near— at the door. 34 Truly I tell you, this generation will certainly not pass away until all these things take place. 35 Heaven and earth will pass away, but my words will never pass away.

Jesus told the disciples to be observant and to be ready for events to unfold. The fig tree illustrated his point. However, this passage is ambiguous and difficult to interpret. Bible scholars have various theories about what Jesus

---

[1] Bonhoeffer, p. 239.

meant.[2] Let us leave aside the controversies and look for applications of the passage to life today.

> [Jesus said:] When evening comes you [Pharisees and Sadducees] say, 'It will be good weather because the sky is red.' And in the morning, 'Today will be stormy because the sky is red and threatening.' You know how to read the appearance of the sky, but you can't read the signs of the times.
>
> Matthew 16:2–3 (CSB)

Meteorologists today may have sophisticated computer models to predict the weather, but you don't need to be an expert to know a thunderstorm is coming when the dark clouds rise into the sky west of my house.

I must be watchful and recognize the spiritual significance of events. The gospel reaching all kinds of people will happen before he comes. Great distress in a locality is a sign that Jesus will surely return. Unusual darkening of heavenly bodies remind us his coming could be at any time.

> Therefore, brothers and sisters, be patient until the Lord's coming. See how the farmer waits for the precious fruit of the earth and is patient with it until it receives the early and the late rains. You also must be patient. Strengthen your hearts, because the Lord's coming is near.
>
> James 5:7–8 (CSB)

After I see flowers, I must be patient for my mangoes to mature. If the rains come on time, I will have an abundant harvest. God is in control of events in my backyard.

I prefer to interpret *this generation* in 24:34 as those alive at the time Jesus spoke.[3] For the disciples who heard Jesus in person, Jesus predicted distress was coming soon to Judea. For us, almost two thousand years later, we are assured God is in control of events. Like the disciples, I must be prepared for distress in my local area. Even though distress may come, Jesus will return at the right time.

> But the day of the Lord will come like a thief; on that day the heavens will pass away with a loud noise, the elements will burn and be dissolved, and the earth and the works on it will be disclosed.
>
> 2 Peter 3:10 (CSB)

---

[2]Carson, pp. 506–507. The translators of the CSB and many commentators assume *near—at the door* in verse 33 refers to the return of Jesus in glory described in verses 29–31, because that is the immediate preceding passage. However, that assumption makes interpreting *this generation* in verse 34 difficult. Other Bible scholars assume that the phrase *all these things* refers to events described in verses 15–22 and that the destruction of Jerusalem will be *near—at the door*. The latter is the interpretation I prefer.

[3]Carson, p. 507. The fall of Jerusalem to the Romans happened about 40 years after Jesus spoke these words. Forty years was the common symbol in ancient Israel for one generation. If one assumes the events surrounding the fall of Jerusalem described in verses 15–22 is what *all these things* refers to in verse 34, then they occurred within one generation, fulfilling Jesus' prophecy.

Modern astronomy has discovered the tremendous size and power of celestial bodies. The destruction of Planet Earth does not seem fanciful anymore. When this world has run its course, God will provide a new heaven and a new earth for believers.[4]

Heaven and earth in 24:35 are representative of all of creation. They seem to be unchanging. Yet Peter prophesied they will pass away. Jesus said his words are even more durable than creation.

The words of the Lord are reliable and his prophecies are sure to come to pass. For example, his prophecy of the destruction of the temple in Jerusalem was fulfilled in AD 70. I know he is reliable, even if I don't understand all the details right now.

The days of Noah

During World War II, keeping the date and place of D-day secret was critically important to the Allies based in Britain. If the Nazis had known, they would have repulsed the invasion. As events played out, God blessed many details of the invasion, including keeping the date and place secret. The heavenly Father has decided to keep the date of Jesus' return secret. Not even the angels or Jesus himself will know until the time comes.

Matthew 24:36–42 (CSB)[5]

---

36 Now concerning that day and hour no one knows—neither the angels of heaven nor the Son—except the Father alone. 37 As the days of Noah were, so the coming of the Son of Man will be. 38 For in those days before the flood they were eating and drinking, marrying and giving in marriage, until the day Noah boarded the ark. 39 They didn't know until the flood came and swept them all away. This is the way the coming of the Son of Man will be. 40 Then two men will be in the field; one will be taken and one left. 41 Two women will be grinding grain with a hand mill; one will be taken and one left. 42 Therefore be alert, since you don't know what day your Lord is coming.

No one knows when Jesus will return. Jesus compared his return to Noah's Flood which took everyone by surprise.

By faith Noah, after he was warned about what was not yet seen and motivated by godly fear, built an ark to deliver his family. By faith he condemned the world and became an heir of the righteousness that comes by faith.

Hebrews 11:7 (CSB)

---

[4]Revelation 21:1.
[5]Luke 17:26–27 is a parallel passage.

People saw Noah build the ark, and may have listened to him preach.[6] They may have seen Noah and his family enter the ark with the animals, yet they were surprised by the flood and were swept away.

When Jesus returns, the public will not be expecting anything different. Even though there will be "birth pains" and distress, everyday life will go on. But suddenly, Jesus will come. I must be alert.

> Above all, be aware of this: Scoffers will come in the last days scoffing and following their own evil desires, saying, "Where is his 'coming' that he promised? Ever since our ancestors fell asleep, all things continue as they have been since the beginning of creation."
>
> 2 Peter 3:3–4 (CSB)

A tornado came through the campus. A large oak tree was uprooted and destroyed. The tree was perhaps twenty feet from the Student Union building on one side and perhaps forty feet from a historic classroom building on the other. Neither building was damaged. Some things get swept away and other things are unscathed.

Worldly powers will resist Jesus' reign as king.[7] Conflict is expected, and we know who will prevail. Some will be swept away by events at the time of Jesus' return. We are not told whether they will be swept away by God's judgment or whether they will be victims of the rebellion by worldly powers.[8] When Jesus returns, others may be preoccupied with daily life, earning a living or making dinner, but I must be alert.

Over the centuries, many have come and gone who have said, "Jesus is coming on such and such day." They and their followers made elaborate preparations, went to some special mountain, and waited and waited. Our passage in Matthew practically guarantees that all who follow such false prophets will be disappointed. The Father knows the right time. I must be alert.

A homeowner

My neighbors were away for the day. When they returned, they found a burglar had carefully gone through their house looking for valuables. The only thing missing was a frozen chicken.

Matthew 24:43–44 (CSB)[9]

---

43 But know this: If the homeowner had known what time the thief was coming, he would have stayed alert and not let his house be

---

[6] 2 Peter 2:5.

[7] Psalm 2:1–3.

[8] Some commentators think *taken* in verses 40–41 refers to the rapture of believers (1 Thessalonians 4:13–18). However, those who were taken in the days of Noah were not believers, so I don't think those taken in the field or taken grinding flour will be believers (1 Thessalonians 5:2–3).

[9] Luke 12:39–40 is a parallel passage.

broken into. 44 This is why you are also to be ready, because the Son of Man is coming at an hour you do not expect.

A burglar plans to steal from a house when no one is home. A homeowner prepares to defend his home no matter when the burglar tries to get in. Believers must be just as prepared as that homeowner.

[Jesus said:] Watch! Be alert! For you don't know when the time is coming.

Mark 13:33 (CSB)

We had an appointment for lunch with friends. They planned to pick us up at our house, but I didn't know exactly when they would arrive. I got dressed and sat down by the front window. In a few minutes, I recognized their car coming down the street. I shouted to my wife, "They're almost here!" and we hurried out to their car.

I must live my life always expecting the return of Jesus. My watchfulness must be like the owner of a house who watches for a burglar to break in. The day and hour of his return will be a surprise to everyone, but those who are always expectant will not be embarrassed, but will be ready to enter his Kingdom.

Stewards

Our friend had a new job almost a thousand miles away. We all worked together to load the truck with furniture and household items. We were almost done when suddenly pizza appeared.

Matthew 24:45–51 (CSB)[10]

45 Who then is a faithful and wise servant, whom his master has put in charge of his household, to give them food at the proper time? 46 Blessed is that servant whom the master finds doing his job when he comes. 47 Truly I tell you, he will put him in charge of all his possessions. 48 But if that wicked servant says in his heart, 'My master is delayed,' 49 and starts to beat his fellow servants, and eats and drinks with drunkards, 50 that servant's master will come on a day he does not expect him and at an hour he does not know. 51 He will cut him to pieces and assign him a place with the hypocrites, where there will be weeping and gnashing of teeth.

It was common in the first century for household slaves to manage a master's affairs. Jesus told this parable of the stewards to teach his disciples what

[10]Luke 12:42–46 is a parallel passage.

they should be doing until he comes, and how his surprise return will result in commendation and condemnation.

> The Lord's servant must not quarrel, but must be gentle to every-one, able to teach, and patient, instructing his opponents with gen-tleness.
>
>   2 Timothy 2:24–25 (CSB)

The parable of the stewards directly applies to Christian leaders. The ones who have affected my spiritual life the most have been leaders of home Bible studies. They knew what spiritual food I needed and their lives were vivid examples. Like the faithful servant, they will be commended for doing what the master assigned them to do. The faithful servant makes sure the other servants receive spiritual food and grow in the faith.

Even though I am eagerly expecting Jesus' return, he does not expect me to go camp out on a mountain top to wait for him. Like the faithful steward, he expects me to lead by example, living the Kingdom lifestyle with gentle-ness and patience, doing the Kingdom mission, keeping a humble Kingdom attitude, and experiencing the power of the Holy Spirit around me. When he returns and finds me engaged in these things, it will be good for me. If a Chris-tian is not faithful, it won't be good.

> [Jesus] answered them, "Isaiah prophesied correctly about you hypocrites, as it is written:
>
>> This people honors me with their lips,
>> but their heart is far from me."
>
>   Mark 7:6 (CSB)

The sign outside said it was a church. Inside the sermons were so filled with anger and criticism that it felt like the pastor was beating the sheep.

An evil steward may flatter the master to his face, but he abuses his author-ity and squanders his master's resources. He thinks he will get away with it. His master's return will surprise him, and the master will execute justice for his evil deeds.

The fate of the evil steward is a warning to leaders of the church today. Those responsible for the care of Jesus' disciples cannot just go through the motions of church on Sunday and expect the returning king to commend them.

Virgins

The wedding guests filed out of the church and gathered at the door to wish the happy couple on their way. We waited... and waited... Why was the pho-tographer taking so many? We waited some more. Suddenly, they appeared in the doorway and ran through the cheering crowd to their car.

Matthew 25:1–13 (CSB)

---

1 At that time the kingdom of heaven will be like ten virgins who took their lamps and went out to meet the groom. 2 Five of them were foolish and five were wise. 3 When the foolish took their lamps, they didn't take oil with them; 4 but the wise ones took oil in their flasks with their lamps. 5 When the groom was delayed, they all became drowsy and fell asleep.

6 In the middle of the night there was a shout: 'Here's the groom! Come out to meet him.'

7 Then all the virgins got up and trimmed their lamps. 8 The foolish ones said to the wise ones, 'Give us some of your oil, because our lamps are going out.'

9 The wise ones answered, 'No, there won't be enough for us and for you. Go instead to those who sell oil, and buy some for yourselves.'

10 When they had gone to buy some, the groom arrived, and those who were ready went in with him to the wedding banquet, and the door was shut. 11 Later the rest of the virgins also came and said, 'Master, master, open up for us!'

12 He replied, 'Truly I tell you, I don't know you!'

13 Therefore be alert, because you don't know either the day or the hour.

This story is set in the context of marriage customs in Jesus' day.[11] The virgins were invited to the wedding banquet and waited outside. The groom was delayed until late at night. The virgins who were prepared for the long delay joined the banquet, but those who were not prepared were shut out.

> The Lord does not delay his promise, as some understand delay, but is patient with you, not wanting any to perish but all to come to repentance.
>
> 2 Peter 3:9 (CSB)

When I was a kid, the ride to my grandparents' house seemed to take forever. It was actually only about an hour and a half. What seemed like a long time to a kid was just a short ride to Mom and Dad.

The parable of the virgins hints that Jesus' return may be delayed longer than some expect. The five foolish virgins were surprised by how long the groom was delayed. The wise virgins were ready for any situation, a quick return or a long delay.

It has been almost two thousand years since Jesus told this story. Many consider this a long delay. Skeptics taunt, "Where is your Messiah?"[12] Peter

---

[11]Carson, p. 513.
[12]2 Peter 3:3–7.

explained why the return of the Lord has been delayed. The heavenly Father wants everyone to repent and receive life. Jesus is sure to arrive when the time is right. We must just wait.

> Dear friends, while you wait for [new heavens and a new earth], make every effort to be found without spot or blemish in his sight, at peace.
>
> 2 Peter 3:14 (CSB)

Some people become so emotionally attached to souvenirs of the past that they can't stand to be separated from them. When Jesus returns, I won't want to take my stuff with me. My personal business won't need a last-minute fix before I go.

Jesus explicitly stated the lesson of the parable of the virgins. Be watchful, because we do not know when he will return. Like the wise virgins, I am ready for him at any time, tomorrow, in twenty years, or if he is delayed even more. My relationship with Jesus is secure and I'm clean.

When is he coming?

When will Jesus return? Will it be in my lifetime? There are many Bible prophecy experts today. They analyze current events for "signs of the times." They say a story in the newspaper or a trend in society is fulfillment of such and such verse of Scripture. The Bible says we are in the "last hour."[13] We can be sure of one thing: everyone will be surprised when Jesus returns.

Only the heavenly Father knows the date. Jesus explained the surprise with several illustrations.

A fig tree. Jesus told the parable of the fig tree. As significant events occur, be ready. Jesus predicted the destruction of the temple which was fulfilled in AD 70 by the Roman siege of Jerusalem. He predicted Judea would suffer great distress at that time. Fulfilled prophecy reassures me that God is in control of world events, no matter how difficult the times may be. I will recognize the spiritual significance of events, even though I don't understand all the details. I must be alert for his return.

The days of Noah. Jesus' return will surprise everyone, just like the flood in Noah's time. Everyone will be doing their normal routine, working a job or making dinner, but I must be alert for his return.

A homeowner. No one knows when Jesus is coming. A burglar doesn't advertise when he will rob a house, so a homeowner must always be ready. I must be alert for Jesus' return.

---

[13] 1 John 2:18.

Stewards. Some people will be living the Kingdom lifestyle when Jesus returns, and others will think they can get away with abusing the faithful. Jesus will surprise the faithful servants with commendation and the wicked with condemnation. I must be alert for his return.

Virgins. Some think a two-thousand-year delay is a long time. The heavenly Father is giving people time to repent. Like a delayed wedding procession, Jesus will arrive at the right time. I won't need to do anything at the last minute to get ready. I must be alert for his return.

When is he coming? Fulfilled prophecies in the past assure me future prophecies will be fulfilled. No one knows when Jesus will return. It will be a surprise, just like Noah's Flood, a burglar, a master returning from a trip, and a wedding procession. I must be alert for his return.

26

After his coming

He who offers a cup of cold water to the weakest and poorest who bears no honourable name has ministered to Christ himself, and Jesus Christ will be his reward.

Dietrich Bonhoeffer[1]

The greatest in the Kingdom of Heaven is the humble disciple. When one offers the most basic hospitality of a drink of cold water to the most humble disciple, it is like offering it to Jesus himself. When Jesus returns he will reward such simple hospitality.

When Jesus returns to earth as king, he will judge all mankind. Believers will have shown compassion to others. They will be surprised when Jesus, the King, commends them, because living the Kingdom lifestyle seemed normal.

Talents

When Angie was a teenager, her mother gave her an allowance which she had to spend on lunches, haircuts, school supplies, tickets for school activities, and gas to go to the beach with friends. She had to manage it carefully.

Matthew 25:14–30 (CSB)[2]

---

14 For it is just like a man about to go on a journey. He called his own servants and entrusted his possessions to them. 15 To one he gave five talents, to another two talents, and to another one talent, depending on each one's ability. Then he went on a journey. Immediately 16 the man who had received five talents went, put them to work, and earned five more. 17 In the same way the man with two

---

[1] Bonhoeffer, p. 246.
[2] Luke 19:12–27 is a similar parable but not a parallel.

earned two more. 18 But the man who had received one talent went off, dug a hole in the ground, and hid his master's money.

19 After a long time the master of those servants came and settled accounts with them. 20 The man who had received five talents approached, presented five more talents, and said, 'Master, you gave me five talents. See, I've earned five more talents.'

21 His master said to him, 'Well done, good and faithful servant! You were faithful over a few things; I will put you in charge of many things. Share your master's joy.'

22 The man with two talents also approached. He said, 'Master, you gave me two talents. See, I've earned two more talents.'

23 His master said to him, 'Well done, good and faithful servant! You were faithful over a few things; I will put you in charge of many things. Share your master's joy.'

24 The man who had received one talent also approached and said, 'Master, I know you. You're a harsh man, reaping where you haven't sown and gathering where you haven't scattered seed. 25 So I was afraid and went off and hid your talent in the ground. See, you have what is yours.'

26 His master replied to him, 'You evil, lazy servant! If you knew that I reap where I haven't sown and gather where I haven't scattered, 27 then you should have deposited my money with the bankers, and I would have received my money back with interest when I returned.

28 'So take the talent from him and give it to the one who has ten talents. 29 For to everyone who has, more will be given, and he will have more than enough. But from the one who does not have, even what he has will be taken away from him. 30 And throw this good-for-nothing servant into the outer darkness, where there will be weeping and gnashing of teeth.'

This passage is traditionally called the *parable of the talents* even though it's about servants. The master in the parable expected his household slaves to invest his money in business. He gave to each steward according to his ability. A *talent* in Roman times was a large amount of money.[3] In modern terms, one talent of silver would be worth about 6,000 times the minimum wage for a day's work.

Two of the three stewards were faithful to invest in business, but one was afraid of losing the money and did not invest it. Like the parable of the virgins,[4] the master returned after a long time.

Paul told Timothy how believers who are rich should manage their wealth.

---

[3]Carson, p. 516.
[4]25:1–13.

> Instruct those who are rich in the present age not to be arrogant
> or to set their hope on the uncertainty of wealth, but on God, who
> richly provides us with all things to enjoy. Instruct them to do what
> is good, to be rich in good works, to be generous and willing to
> share, storing up treasure for themselves as a good foundation for
> the coming age, so that they may take hold of what is truly life.
>
> 1 Timothy 6:17–19 (CSB)

I noticed the sermon topic was going to be about finances. Attendance was down that Sunday. I overheard someone say, "The preacher is meddling again." Most people don't want anyone to tell them what to do with their money.

Watching for the return of Jesus is not a passive hobby. I will invest what the Lord has given me, but just giving money to Christian organizations is not enough. I will follow Paul's instructions. Don't be arrogant. Don't be materialistic. Do good. Be generous. I know opportunities to be generous occur every day. I will be busy doing my Savior's business, namely, living the Kingdom lifestyle, doing the Kingdom mission, and keeping a humble Kingdom attitude no matter what I am doing.

> And whatever you do, in word or in deed, do everything in the
> name of the Lord Jesus, giving thanks to God the Father through
> him.
>
> Colossians 3:17 (CSB)

What are applications of the *talents* in this parable? Jesus has given me many things he expects me to use until he comes. The most obvious application is my money. I am responsible to use whatever money comes through my hands in the Kingdom way. This includes providing for my family, ordinary expenses of life, giving to Kingdom causes, and even investing in business.

Another application of *talents* is my skills and abilities. For example, my guitar playing should be done for the Lord. The same is true for other skills and abilities.

Another application of *talents* is material things I have. For example, my car can provide transportation for Kingdom purposes. I gave regular rides to church to a friend who didn't have a car. The fellowship on the way was more valuable than the cost of transportation.

Whenever I find I'm not using a household item, I'm glad to give it to someone who will enjoy using it. For example, my wife and I gave a big box of cookbooks to a new bride. At our age, the recipes were too fattening for us to use.

Life does not consist of storing, cleaning, and maintaining stuff. Using stuff in Kingdom life is what really counts. Investing my talents means everything I do must be done as a servant of Jesus. I am thankful for the stuff he provides and for the privilege to represent him.

Sheep and goats

Each spring, mangoes ripen on the two trees in my backyard. Day after day, I collect the ones that fall to the ground. Some will be half eaten by raccoons. Some will have a bite taken by squirrels. Some will be rotten. Some will too small. Some will be too green. Others will be good after ripening a few days on the kitchen counter. I must judge whether each mango is good or bad. After Jesus comes, he will judge mankind.

Matthew 25:31–46 (CSB)

---

31 When the Son of Man comes in his glory, and all the angels with him, then he will sit on his glorious throne. 32 All the nations will be gathered before him, and he will separate them one from another, just as a shepherd separates the sheep from the goats. 33 He will put the sheep on his right and the goats on the left.

34 Then the King will say to those on his right, 'Come, you who are blessed by my Father; inherit the kingdom prepared for you from the foundation of the world. 35 For I was hungry and you gave me something to eat; I was thirsty and you gave me something to drink; I was a stranger and you took me in; 36 I was naked and you clothed me; I was sick and you took care of me; I was in prison and you visited me.'

37 Then the righteous will answer him, 'Lord, when did we see you hungry and feed you, or thirsty and give you something to drink? 38 When did we see you a stranger and take you in, or without clothes and clothe you? 39 When did we see you sick, or in prison, and visit you?'

40 And the King will answer them, 'Truly I tell you, whatever you did for one of the least of these brothers and sisters of mine, you did for me.'

41 Then he will also say to those on the left, 'Depart from me, you who are cursed, into the eternal fire prepared for the devil and his angels! 42 For I was hungry and you gave me nothing to eat; I was thirsty and you gave me nothing to drink; 43 I was a stranger and you didn't take me in; I was naked and you didn't clothe me, sick and in prison and you didn't take care of me.'

44 Then they too will answer, 'Lord, when did we see you hungry, or thirsty, or a stranger, or without clothes, or sick, or in prison, and not help you?'

45 Then he will answer them, 'I tell you, whatever you did not do for one of the least of these, you did not do for me.'

46 And they will go away into eternal punishment, but the righteous into eternal life.

The setting for this passage is clearly after Jesus has returned and claimed his kingdom on earth. The judgment scene will be similar to a shepherd separating sheep and goats. The disciples were familiar with how shepherds let sheep and goats mingle in a pasture and later separated them. John had a similar vision of the judgment of mankind.

> Then I saw a great white throne and one seated on it. Earth and heaven fled from his presence, and no place was found for them. I also saw the dead, the great and the small, standing before the throne, and books were opened. Another book was opened, which is the book of life, and the dead were judged according to their works by what was written in the books. Then the sea gave up the dead that were in it, and death and Hades gave up the dead that were in them; each one was judged according to their works.
>
> Revelation 20:11–13 (CSB)

This passage depicts what happened in John's vision to those whose names were not in the book of life. Believers' names were in the book of life, but the names of unbelievers were missing. People were judged based on what they had done in this life. Their punishment was portrayed as a fiery lake. The message is clear even though presented with imagery.

The Scriptures are clear that the criterion for eternal life is faith in Jesus. The good works of the sheep and goats, or their omission, will be evidence of destiny, not the cause of destiny.[5] The king's criterion also will test for hypocrisy.[6] The sheep genuinely loved one another. The goats were indifferent. If a goat claims to be a Christian, his actions will belie that claim.

The sheep and goats will not expect their works to be significant. The recipients were not important people in society. Jesus considers the most humble person in the Kingdom to be the greatest, so good works toward such citizens of the Kingdom are reckoned to be just as important as good works toward Jesus the king himself.[7]

Paul assured the Colossians that service for the Lord will result in a heavenly inheritance.

> Whatever you do, do it from the heart, as something done for the Lord and not for people, knowing that you will receive the reward of an inheritance from the Lord. You serve the Lord Christ. For the wrongdoer will be paid back for whatever wrong he has done, and there is no favoritism.
>
> Colossians 3:23–25 (CSB)

When my mother died, I inherited the house my parents had owned. It was fully equipped for a homeowner. As a citizen of the Kingdom of Heaven, I have a secure fully equipped inheritance that goes with eternal life.

---

[5]Carson, p. 521.

[6]Carson, p. 522.

[7]18:4–5.

God has been planning the Kingdom of Heaven since the beginning and he will bring it to fulfillment under the reign of Jesus. Righteousness, peace, and joy will be its hallmarks.[8] Wicked and lazy servants will be excluded. Compassionate servants will be welcomed. If I practice the Kingdom lifestyle now, I will be ready to live in the eternal Kingdom then, standing with the Lord's other sheep.

After his coming

When a business goes bankrupt, the court clears away bad debts and a renewed company often emerges. The previous management is usually fired. A new manager comes in who must determine who will have jobs in the renewed company. This world is sinking deeper and deeper in sin. It is spiritually bankrupt. The heavenly Father has appointed Jesus to be the new manager.

After Jesus comes to earth, he will tend to some unfinished business. He will separate believers and unbelievers. He will judge everyone for what they have done, and believers, in particular, will be judged for how they have used what he has given them.

Talents. The parable of the talents contrasts three stewards of their master's money. When their master returned from a long trip, he found two had been faithful and so they were rewarded. But one did not invest his master's money as he was instructed, and was severely punished. Similarly, Jesus will return after being away for a couple of thousand years. He will ask me what have I done with what he gave me. My goal is to be like the faithful servants in the parable. While he is away, I will invest in the Kingdom what he has given me, not only money, but also my skills and possessions.

Sheep and goats. After Jesus returns, he will judge all mankind for what they have done. Jesus will separate his followers from the rebel allies of the devil like a shepherd separates sheep from goats. The names of believers will be in the book of life.[9] Their lives will exhibit compassion for humble disciples in need. The lives of the rebels will exhibit selfishness and hatred for Jesus' disciples. Neither the sheep nor the goats will think their actions were significant, but King Jesus will consider them just as important as good works toward himself.

After his coming. On judgment day, Jesus will evaluate me for my stewardship over what he has given me. The illustration of the sheep and the goats shows me how the Lord will evaluate my life. Did I show compassion toward his humble disciples? How I live my life now will matter after Jesus returns to earth.

---

[8]Romans 14:17.
[9]Revelation 20:11–13.

27

The coming of the king

In the end the whole world must bow before [the will of God], worshipping, and giving thanks in joy and tribulation. Heaven and earth shall be subject to God.

Dietrich Bonhoeffer[1]

When Jesus, the King, comes, I will worship with Bonhoeffer and all the other believers around the throne. I won't remember any persecution or distress of the past, and all of creation will be redeemed from the curse of sin.

At the beginning of this discourse, the disciples wanted answers. When will the temple be destroyed? What will be the sign of your coming as Messiah? What will be the sign of the end of the age?

Before his coming. Ever since Jesus ascended, there has been turmoil, persecution, distress, and false messiahs. Jesus predicted great distress in Judea which was fulfilled by the siege of Jerusalem and the destruction of the temple by the Romans in AD 70. The turmoil and distress mean the true messiah is coming, but not yet.

His coming. The undeniable sign of his coming is the personal appearance of Jesus himself in the clouds. His coming will not be a secret.

Jesus, the King, will return to earth with power and glory. After Jesus ascended to heaven, angels told the disciples he will personally return.[2]

When is he coming? Even though people try to discern the "signs of the times," no one knows when Jesus is coming. It will be a surprise. I must be ready for his coming.

---

[1] Bonhoeffer, p. 185.
[2] Acts 1:9–11.

191

After his coming. What will happen when Jesus returns?

> The kingdom of the world has become the kingdom
> of our Lord and of his Christ,
> and he will reign forever and ever.
>
> Revelation 11:15 (CSB)

Not only does the Kingdom of Heaven refer to a current spiritual reality, but when Jesus returns he will take over from earthly kings, leaders, and governments.[3] Jesus rules the citizens of the Kingdom now. The unbelievers are rebels. In the end, Jesus, the king, will enforce his rule over all, including the leaders of all the nations.

Jesus will require an accounting by his disciples for what they have done with the resources he has given them. He will also judge everyone for what they have done. The rebels will face condemnation.

How long will the Kingdom of Heaven last? I was amazed when I visited the site of the terracotta warriors in China. Thousands of life-size sculptures of soldiers were buried in the tomb of Qin Shi Huang, the first emperor of China, in about 210 BC. His tomb was an indication of the splendor of his reign. But his kingdom did not last. Another dynasty took over a few years after his death.

> [The godly] will speak of the glory of your kingdom
> and will declare your might,
> informing all people of your mighty acts
> and of the glorious splendor of your kingdom.
> Your kingdom is an everlasting kingdom;
> your rule is for all generations.
> The Lord is faithful in all his words
> and gracious in all his actions.
>
> Psalm 145:11–13 (CSB)

Human civilizations rise and fall. Archaeologists have discovered the ruins of ancient civilizations all over the world. They no longer exist. One might ask whether the Kingdom of Heaven will be any different. The Bible promises the Kingdom of Heaven will last forever. The eternal God guarantees it.[4]

I'm eager to see Jesus personally. His reign will bring justice and righteousness to the earth.

---

[3]Philippians 2:9–11 and Revelation 1:5.
[4]Luke 1:33.

28

The Kingdom of Heaven is near

In the world the Christians are a colony of the true home, they are strangers and aliens in a foreign land, enjoying the hospitality of that land, obeying its laws and honouring its government.

Dietrich Bonhoeffer[1]

The Kingdom of Heaven lifestyle is not like the world's. Citizens of the Kingdom don't fit into their wild parties and vicious business practices. Citizens believe God's Word, put it into practice, look for the king's return, and do the good works God has prepared.[2]

The Kingdom of Heaven was God's plan from the beginning. The Law and Prophets were witnesses to his sovereignty. Jesus is the king over the Kingdom of Heaven. His resurrection from the dead validated his authority.

> [God] has rescued us from the domain of darkness and transferred us into the kingdom of the Son he loves.
>
> Colossians 1:13 (CSB)

I don't have to wait for the Kingdom. I'm already in the Kingdom of Heaven. God has forgiven my sins and redeemed my life. I'm no longer a citizen of Satan's kingdom of darkness. God has made me a citizen of his kingdom of light. How then should a citizen of the Kingdom of Heaven live? Jesus taught his disciples what to do. Each of the discourses of Jesus in Matthew's gospel addresses a question about the Kingdom of Heaven.

- What is the Kingdom of Heaven lifestyle? (5:1–7:29)

- What is the mission of disciples? (10:1–42)

---

[1] Bonhoeffer, p. 303.
[2] Bonhoeffer, p. 334.

- What is the Kingdom of Heaven like? (13:1–52)

- Who is the greatest in the Kingdom of Heaven? (18:1–35)

- What will be the signs of Jesus' coming as king? (24:1–25:46)

The discourses of Jesus in Matthew's gospel teach me basic truths about the Kingdom of Heaven. I will apply the answers to my life, so I can live as a citizen of the Kingdom of Heaven should.

Lifestyle. I am living in the Kingdom now.

> I delight to do your will, my God,
> and your instruction is deep within me.
>
> Psalm 40:8 (CSB)

Whatever the king says is what I want. If the Word of God is in my heart and I resolve to always obey to the best of my knowledge and ability, then I will consistently do what he asks me to do. Studying God's Word will tell me what the Kingdom of Heaven is all about. I'll let his Word go deep in my heart, so I can obey him.

Mission. Believers have a mission to proclaim the Kingdom of Heaven to everyone in spite of persecution.

> For we are his workmanship, created in Christ Jesus for good works, which God prepared ahead of time for us to do.
>
> Ephesians 2:10 (CSB)

God's mission for me is to do the good things he has already planned for me. Sometimes I will explain the Kingdom message. Sometimes only my actions will tell the Kingdom message. God's power will validate the message. I'll do the mission he has assigned to me.

Understanding. God has given me wisdom and understanding.

> In [Jesus] we have redemption through his blood, the forgiveness of our trespasses, according to the riches of his grace that he richly poured out on us with all wisdom and understanding.
>
> Ephesians 1:7–8 (CSB)

Jesus' parables make sense to me, because I am experiencing the Kingdom. I am part of a world-wide community of faith. I understand the dynamics of the Kingdom and people's reactions to the Kingdom message. I learn such things through studying the Bible.

Humility. The greatest in the Kingdom of Heaven is humble like a child.

> All of you clothe yourselves with humility toward one another, be-
> cause
>
>> God resists the proud
>> but gives grace to the humble.
>
> 1 Peter 5:5 (CSB)

My attitude must be humble, not arrogant. I'll be reconciled to my brother whenever a relationship is broken. I'll forgive over and over so I lose count.

His coming. Jesus will return in person to rule over the earth and demonstrate the Kingdom of Heaven to all.

> For you yourselves know very well that the day of the Lord will
> come just like a thief in the night.
> 1 Thessalonians 5:2 (CSB)

We know the return of Jesus will be a surprise to most people. Even though I don't know the day or the hour, I'll always be ready for his coming. Understanding the Kingdom of Heaven prepares me for that day.

Index

About the author

Edward B. Allen is the author of books for three styles of devotional Bible study. Verse-by-verse books draw devotional points from the Scripture passage in sequence. Historical-people books focus on incidents in the lives of historical people that illustrate biblical principles. Topical books explore relevant Scriptures throughout the Bible. His books also include many personal stories from modern life.

His books are in two series. Books in the *A Slow Walk* series have short meditations in daily-devotional format, such as *A Slow Walk through Psalm 119: 90 Devotional Meditations*. Books in the *Devotional Commentary* series are straight reads with a devotional slant, rather than academic or theological comments, such as *Practical Faith: A Devotional Commentary*.

He has led discussion Bible-study groups in evangelical churches for over 50 years He received a Ph.D. in Computer Science degree at Florida Atlantic University and had a career in software engineering. He has authored or coauthored over 80 professional papers.